The *YANKEE*® Way
to Simplify Your Life

The *YANKEE* Way to Simplify Your Life

OLD-FASHIONED WISDOM FOR A NEW-FANGLED WORLD

Jay Heinrichs
and the editors of *Yankee* magazine

William Morrow and Company, Inc.
New York

It is the policy of William Morrow and Company, Inc., and its imprints and affiliates, recognizing the importance of preserving what has been written, to print the books we publish on acid-free paper, and we exert our best efforts to that end.

Library of Congress Cataloging-in-Publication Data
Heinrichs, Jay.
The Yankee way to simplify your life : old-fashioned wisdom for a new-fangled world / Jay Heinrichs and the editors of Yankee magazine.
p.   cm.
Includes index.
ISBN 0-688-14186-2
1. Simplicity.   2. Conduct of life.   3. Self-realization.   4. Life.
I. Yankee magazine.   II. Title.
BJ1496.H45   1996
179'.9—dc20   96-11152
CIP

Printed in the United States of America
First Edition
1   2   3   4   5   6   7   8   9   10
BOOK DESIGN BY EUGENIE SEIDENBERG DELANEY

To Harriet Beecher Stowe, who wrote
great literature to feed her children

Preface

———>●<———

THE STONE WALL

THE WALL LIES HIGH on the Lambert Ridge in New Hampshire. An-
choring a forest of birch and maple, it testifies to an old Yankee
strength.

You have to climb a steep slope for a mile to see the wall, the relic of
an eighteenth-century hill farm. You wonder how the people survived up
there. The land seems more stone than soil. To use it meant removing the
rocks—the great waste product of New England hill farming.

Instead of taking the rocks to a dump, the farmers made walls, divid-
ing pasture and keeping livestock in bounds. The work is not easy, especially
on a slope. The rocks are heavy, and the flies are hungry.

Still, the walls got built, and they lasted. Look down to the rich bot-
tomlands along New England rivers; there is little trace of the original
farms. It was the hill farmers who took the rocks and built a legacy.

Moral: When we do more than dispose of our obstacles, when we build
something from what stands in our way, we learn a secret from the Yankees of old.

We learn what it is to simplify.

Acknowledgments

————————

I T IS CUSTOMARY to thank people without whose help a book would be impossible. Bill Adler certainly falls into that category; this book was his idea. I am grateful to Sharon Smith for thinking of me as the writer, and for acting as lead cheerleader/skeptic. Jamie Trowbridge of *Yankee,* who was to the Puritan manner born, provided moral encouragement (and an occasional moral); William Morrow's Toni Sciarra edited with Yankee-like wisdom. Nancy Trafford offered the unflagging support that every author and self-improver needs.

My family—Dorothy Sr., Dorothy Jr., and George—did much more than put up with an author. They helped write the book. If there are flaws in it, I hope they improve the opportunity and write a better one.

Contents

Introduction

A Personal Tale of Nearly Disastrous Self-improvement

OR A SHORT TIME WHILE WRITING THIS BOOK, I thought that simplifying my life might ruin it. Something seemed to go wrong with whatever aspect of living I happened to be writing about.

The first time it happened I was drafting the passage on the importance of "quantity time" with your kids when my ten-year-old daughter, Dorothy Jr., burst in. "The Bacons are taking me skiing," she said. "Can you come with us, Dad?"

"Beat it, kid," I said. "I'm telling how to be a good parent." Dorothy Jr. moped off and skied without me.

The very next day I was taking notes on how to argue effectively with your spouse when my wife, Dorothy Sr., and I had one of our biggest arguments in years—about Cub Scouts, I think. I ended up sleeping in my home office right next to my notes about simplifying marriage. In the middle of the money section in Chapter 10 some freelance business I'd been counting on fell through. That was followed by an office crisis while I was writing the work chapter. Then I lost my seven-year-old son, George, on New Hampshire's Mount Cardigan for an hour. He had charged on ahead of me and taken a different path. Guess what chapter I was working on? The one on play.

Call it "Self-improvement He Wrote." The very act of writing about simplifying your life seemed to be complicating mine. I became uncharacteristically superstitious, delaying work on Chapter 13, the one about the body, for fear of contracting some deadly disease.

Of course I didn't. It eventually occurred to me that I wasn't messing up my life, I was examining it. Screwups that happen all the time were just becoming more apparent. I was acting like a good Puritan, turning over the soil. Besides, the daily complications of my life proved how qualified I was to talk about simplifying.

My own attempt to simplify my life began a little more than a decade ago, when my wife and I decided to move out of the Washington, D.C., area. The one self-improvement habit we practiced back then was to go on a long walk every New Year's Day and talk about our lives. On this particular ramble I pictured an idyllic little college town in northern New England. She described staying home and caring for two children until she felt like returning to work. We strolled and mooned and then returned to reality.

A few weeks later a man offered me a job in downtown Washington. I thanked him and turned it down. "You can't stay in your job forever," he said. "What do you want to do?"

"I like what I'm doing now," I replied. "But since you asked . . ." and with a somewhat embarrassed smile I told him all about my squirrelly little vision.

"I'm a graduate of Dartmouth College," he said, "and there's an opening there for your sort of work."

I applied and got the job. My wife and I bought a house on ten acres a brisk bike ride from my office. Paths through our land hook up to the twenty-two-hundred-mile Appalachian Trail. I can walk north for twenty-five miles without crossing a paved road. When my wife isn't helping to run our little town, she is home with the kids. We're living our squirrelly little vision.

The day the call came telling me I had the job, the first real moral ever to occur to me suddenly popped into my head. It's not a profound moral, but it's true:

Sometimes you only have to know what you want.

My desire became fate, an outcome that fell into my lap without any goals, habits, targets, or deadlines. All I needed was a timely answer to a friendly man's question.

Since then I've met countless other people who have found a calling just by expressing it. Margo, a colleague at Dartmouth, once decided to spend much of the rest of her life traveling. She didn't have a whole lot of money but nonetheless envisioned a borrowed house in the south of France. Two weeks after she started dreaming in detail she came across a classified ad offering a house swap: a month in a cottage in Provence in return for a month someplace in Vermont. Margo happens to live in Vermont. The swap was a great success that led to more house-swap contacts, and Margo now frugally lives overseas during every bit of vacation time.

Stories like Margo's and mine have led me to believe that our lives actually can improve.

But it is one thing to dream your fate and another to tempt it. I never for a moment thought that my job offer was anything more than dumb luck. I learned that I could let my life change; it took me longer to discover I could improve it on my own. To do that, I had to undergo a process of Yankeefication, shedding my city ways and acquiring some of the attitudes of rural New England. That's another weird story.

Our land is in an area I had never visited before coming north, yet the moment I saw the place it felt familiar. The features had names I seemed to remember: Mink Brook, Goose Pond, Moose Mountain. I was beginning to think there was something to this business about past lives. Then one day I read a profile on the writer Corey Ford, who had lived in New Hampshire and written funny stories during the 1950s and early sixties for *Field and Stream* magazine. Ford invented a group of outdoorsmen called the Lower Forty Shooting, Angling and Inside Straight Club, in a fictional town called Hardscrabble. Turns out Ford modeled Hardscrabble after the very town I had moved to. I suddenly remembered reading *Field and Stream* in barbershops when I was a boy in Philadelphia. The residents of Hardscrabble had seemed to me then to live in a paradise, and for the rest of my life, even after I'd forgotten the stories themselves, I wanted to move to northern New England. I ended up buying land right under Moose Mountain in "Hardscrabble" itself.

That discovery inspired me to read about local history, and I branched out into biographies of old Yankees. I was surprised to find some common traits among the early residents of this region, including their belief in a person's ability to improve.

So I was inspired to try some improvement of my own by transforming myself into a morning person. Imitating nearly every admirable New Englander I'd read about, I devised a scheme to get up at 5:00 every weekday morning (you can see the plan in Chapter 6). I made a pact with myself to stand up automatically before the alarm watch stopped beeping (it has a long beep). I set a new habit of doing calisthenics and stretching first thing. Push-ups at 5:00 A.M. seemed masochistic at first, but we don't heat our house at night, and the exercise warmed me up better than the shower did. I actually started getting used to the routine. On some dark mornings I would find myself on the floor doing push-ups with no clue to how I'd arrived there. On the other hand, it took awhile to get used to actually thinking early in the morning. At times I found myself dozing over my work. But after a while even that got easier. And there was an added benefit: Sleeping in during the weekend meant getting up at 6:30 at the latest, which offered more time to play outside.

I was so proud of myself that I started setting other small goals: to run mountain trails, take more hikes with my children, exhibit more habits of grace with my wife, drink less beer, learn rock climbing. I'm far from meeting some of the goals, as my wife will be the first to tell you. But I'm better off than when I started. I have more time. Nice clothing and new cars and other fashion items seem less important than my more serious acquisitions of habit and physical ability. Even travel seems less of a big deal; a good mountain run is more exciting to me now than a trip to a city, because the mountain seems more attached to my desires. Most of all, I have begun to acquire that quintessential Yankee sense of superiority—not toward others but toward my former slovenly self.

My self-improvement passion has affected the rest of my family in different ways. At the age of forty-one Dorothy Sr. now runs the Appalachian Trail with a friend, and people say she looks twenty-five. Dorothy Jr. has developed goals to improve as a competitive cross-country skier. On the other hand, the day before George's seventh birthday Dorothy Sr. said to him, "You only have twenty-four hours left to be a six-year-old!" George paused on the stairs, stuck a sarcastic forefinger into the air, and said, "I will use the time wisely."

Every family needs a skeptic.

CHAPTER 1

The Simple Life

Regarding what makes a Yankee a Yankee

WHEN WE THINK OF A STEREOTYPICAL YANKEE, certain terms come to mind: plain speaking, ingenuity, hard work, stern morals. If we study them the right way, we can learn a thing or two from Yankees about making life more livable. The early New Englanders knew when and how to be satisfied. They rarely felt sorry for themselves. They had a clear sense of place and how they fitted into it. They knew that everything, especially themselves, can stand improvement.

Not all Yankees were that admirable, of course. Right from the start New England has included the gloriously fat, the lazy, the apartment-bound city dweller. But there is a grain of truth in the more rigorous stereotype. "Yankee" and "simple" go well together for a reason. The first New Englanders took pride in their unornamented religion, speech, writing, dress, and government—simplicity that arose from the basic Puritan virtues of austerity, hard work, and denial of the flesh.

Austerity? Denial? Frankly, to want to return to the days of the Puritans, you'd have to be a little crazy. If instead you can just capture some old-time simplicity, you can become like John Adams, who, while still in his twenties, discovered heaven. Adams was traveling along the Connecticut River toward Hartford when he suddenly came across his idea of paradise on earth, which he duly noted in his diary: "The land will yield two crops of English grass, and two tons and a half at each crop with plenty of after-feed besides, if nicely managed and properly dunged."

Dung? In heaven?

Forget angels and lyres and heathen nectar; Adams's paradise looks a lot like home.

Which leads to two obvious questions: Why would anyone want to be a Yankee? Who wants to plow through the afterlife?

THE MOST PRODUCTIVE YANKEES

ADAMS WASN'T JUST A FARMER, of course; he was one of the most versatile of all American leaders. Throughout history there have been a number of people who, like him, led enormously complex lives and made them look simple. How could Ralph Waldo Emerson lead a grueling speaking schedule, write reams of poetry, and become the leading philosopher of his day? How could Daniel Webster draw crowds of fifty thousand, become the nation's top trial lawyer, and act as one of our greatest diplomats—all at the same time? How on earth did a runaway Boston apprentice named Benjamin Franklin juggle a printing business, studies of electricity, numerous inventions, political theories, best-selling books, and diplomacy while helping to foment American independence? Most impressive of all, how did Harriet Beecher Stowe write *Uncle Tom's Cabin* and help turn an entire nation against slavery while her six children were doing their homework practically on top of her?

If you read up on these and other amazingly productive people, you will discover that nearly all of them had several advantages in common:

1. Servants
2. Wealth
3. Understanding spouses

That leaves out a good many readers of this book, no doubt.

But then, what if it is possible to be more productive without the servants or money? (Understanding spouses have been rare in any century.) What if you could just spend less time on the parts of the day that don't make you any healthier, wealthier, or wiser—like getting up in the morning, commuting to work, sitting in meetings, fixing meals, watching television? How could you find more time for the things you love most—like playing with your kids, hooking a rug, or reading? And how could you have time left over for transcending your usual existence—by learning a new sport, or volunteering, or exploring the world?

The fact is, there are ways to do these things. They can be summed up as the simple life.

The simple life is a busy life, but one in which the pleasurable tasks far outnumber the odious ones. It is a life in which you make progress toward your most important goals and push the less important ones farther back.

In short, the simple life entails knowing the life you really want to live and then living it.

As Henry David Thoreau said, it means getting yourself out from under the details. That does not necessarily mean living like a hermit, wearing

Nostalgia the Way It Used to Be

PHYSICIANS ONCE DIAGNOSED a yearning for the past as a mental disease that could lead to severe weight loss or even suicide. Nostalgia first seemed to afflict seventeenth-century Swiss mercenaries when they were far from home. Dr. Johannes Hofer coined the term from the Greek *nostos* (to return home) and *algia* (pain). He determined the cause to be "the quite continuous vibration of animal spirits through those fibers of the middle brain in which impressed traces of ideas of the Fatherland still cling." Some scientists thought atmospheric pressure was to blame. Swiss soldiers coming down out of the Alps to fight in the flatlands contracted the ailment when they subjected their bodies to greater atmospheric pressure. Up until the early nineteenth century doctors thought the disease was unique to the Swiss. Then other troops began suffering from it. During the American Civil War medics attributed traumatic stress disorder, or shell shock, to nostalgia.

Moral: You can't go "home" to the early New England of our imagination; you risk contracting nostalgia just by yearning for it. But with the help of this book you can reproduce some of the comforts and disciplines of our bygone small-town past.

homespun, and going without electricity or telephone. Some people do just that, of course, but their lives seem rather complicated—not to mention inconvenient, which is saying much the same thing. *You* try rearing babies without running water.

Look at two friends, Jim and Bob.

THE STORY OF JIM AND BOB

SOME YEARS AGO Jim bought a tiny island on a lake in New Hampshire and built a log cabin on it with his own hands. He paddled a canoe to his car when the lake wasn't frozen. When it was, he skated. (When the ice was thin, he took his chances, falling in every now and then.) Inside his cabin were a gas refrigerator, a composting toilet, a woodstove, some wooden furniture, kerosene lamps, and some books. Many people would find Jim's life extremely complicated. He couldn't just pop around the corner for groceries. The temperature in his cabin would be forty degrees when he got home from work in the winter. Yet Jim lived simply—for Jim. He had exactly what he wanted for that time in his life: the outdoors, books, solitude, a couple of fine rocking chairs. He paid no mortgage, he never mowed his lawn (the island is covered entirely with blueberry bushes), and good swimming and fishing were right at his doorstep. While Jim doesn't live on the island anymore, he has not exactly moved to suburbia. He is restoring an eighteenth-century farmhouse that has never known electricity, and Jim, being Jim, has no intention of introducing it.

To Jim, his country life is simple. But Jim's friend Bob lives just as simply in the city. Bob moved from New Hampshire to live in a small Manhattan apartment and work as the entertainment editor of a big magazine. He has traveled all over the world, wears a killer double-breasted suit ("Hey!" he says. "It's Manhattan"), and accompanies his wife, a New York banker, to shows or parties or expensive restaurants almost every night. He doesn't have a car; he walks to work or takes a cab. He is an abominable cook, and he cheerfully keeps his refrigerator almost entirely empty. (Hey! It's Manhattan. He eats out.) He keeps in shape by running to the office through Central Park and has time for almost everything he wants to do.

While Jim and Bob have many similarities, neither would be caught dead living the other's life. These two guys show that there is no one simple life. The simple life is what is simple *for you.*

The simple life means creatively narrowing your choices so they don't overwhelm you.

It means having *time*—time to stay caught up with work, time to think about the future, time for your loved ones, time for yourself.

It means eating what you want, and not what your cravings force you to eat.

It means having enough money and possessions to live the way you want and being reasonably satisfied with what you have.

HOW DO YOU KNOW
IF YOU'RE LIVING SIMPLY?

I F YOU CAN SAY YES to each of these questions, yours is the simple life. If the answer to any or all of them is no, well . . . that's what this book is for.

1. Do you know exactly what you want out of life?
2. Do you have enough time during the day or week or year to do what you want?
3. Do your habits lead to goals?

As the next chapter shows, the early New Englanders were the first to come up with organized answers to those three questions. The aim should be to lead not the life of some old Yankee—just your own. But it doesn't take much to figure out that that can be the toughest, and the most rewarding, feat of all.

Eight Basic Morals to the Yankee Story

Throughout this book you will find many morals, but they can be boiled down to eight essential ones (to simplify, you have to boil down). Some of them may not make perfect sense to you, but don't worry. If everything were explained right here, what would be the point of reading this book?

1. **Ignore the silver lining. Use the cloud.** Some of your greatest opportunities come from obstacles. Later we'll talk about the advantages of lowered expectations, bad habits, and noble failures.
2. **It's hard to set a course when you don't know where you are.** Our lives are complicated by the crosscurrents that buffet them. A couple of chapters will help you establish a sense of place and a sense of self.
3. **A well-chosen goal looks a lot like fate.** It is much simpler to meet a goal that seems inevitable than one that appears unattainable. We'll go into useful Puritan beliefs that helped inspire the Yankee approach to living.
4. **A wide target is easier to hit than a narrow one.** Goals often fail because they are hard to measure. This book will show you how to set the right goals and stay inspired by them.
5. **If the road to hell is paved with good intentions, the road to heaven is paved with habits.** The good habit is the best way to get free from the morass of day-to-day details. You will learn how to establish a habit and how to make a bad one serve you.

(continued on next page)

6. **Pleasure has more stamina than duty.** We mess up our lives when we swim against our own current.

7. **When you count your blessings, round up.** The best way to simplify is to know when, and how, to be satisfied. This book will help you use the techniques of artillery officers to "bracket" your expectations.

8. **Do nothing to excess, including doing nothing to excess.** "Simplify, simplify," wrote Thoreau, himself using twice as many words as he had to. He was a wise man who avoided simplifying to the point of complication.

CHAPTER 2

The Puritan Secret

In which is revealed the Yankee's
most ingenious invention: the Yankee

I F YOU DOUBT THAT YOU CAN SIMPLIFY YOUR LIFE, join the crowd. Although Americans spend billions of dollars a year in attempts to improve themselves—the diet industry alone rakes in thirty-three billion—it is unfashionable actually to believe that we can improve. Are we unhappy? Our childhood and parents are much to blame, and we can't fix *them*. Are we caught in the web of terrible habits? It's our addictive personality. Are we in debt to our credit cards and car companies? That's part of being an American. We even blame our faults on strange mental diseases. A woman recently brought her son to New Hampshire neurologist Richard Nordgren and announced that the boy was a lousy student because he had "work output deficit disorder." The mother had not made a new medical discovery. She had lost something, a faith that got its start in New England and helped create an unprecedented burst of energy and wealth.

The secret behind the success of the Puritans was their belief in everyone's ability, even duty, to improve. They loved to tell the story of the Old Testament prophet Jeremiah, who one day visited a potter. The craftsman messed up a pot he was making, but instead of throwing it away he took the same clay and remolded it. At that point the voice of God popped into Jeremiah's head: "Have not I the right to deal with men and with nations as this potter has dealt with this clay?" (Think of Jeremiah when you despair of changing your own shape.)

The Puritans reshaped themselves with the help of some simple principles:

Examine thyself. Early New Englanders often took perverse pleasure in listing, and sometimes exaggerating, their faults. But they did it for a reason. By studying their faults, they hoped to learn how to eliminate them. They also gained useful self-awareness. In the next chapter we'll complete an important exercise in self-examination. Not being Puritans ourselves, we'll cover pleasures and admirable traits as well as faults.

Everyone is improvable. Regardless of family, childhood, or obstacles, a person could end up as one of the elect, especially favored by God. All it took, the Puritans thought, was a good education and the grace of the Almighty.

Every opportunity is an obligation. The Puritans, who believed in a strangely energetic form of predestination, taught that God gives you a set of innate abilities and then provides the circumstances for carrying them out. It is up to you to "improve your opportunities." If you work hard and do well, then your behavior might reveal you as one of the elect. On the other hand, if you blow your chances, you are probably one of those poor souls destined for hell. Some people have it in them; some don't. Needless to say, Puritans fell over one another trying to prove they had it in them.

A Town Not Named Dukakis

➤●◄

ADAMS, NEW HAMPSHIRE, changed its name to Jackson when Andrew Jackson beat John Quincy Adams in the 1828 election. The town had first been named in 1800, when John Adams won the presidency.

Moral: To a good Yankee, every event is an improvable moment.

Good things come from good habits. Early New Englanders knew how to set their lives on autopilot by establishing useful routines. One old Yankee technique allowed extraordinary accomplishments: the habit of getting up at five. In Chapter 6, I'll talk about why that's such an advantage (and how you can gain it, if you dare).

It's all right to feel a bit superior. What made early New Englanders hardest to bear also helped make them extraordinarily productive people. It was everyone's duty to believe that he or she was one of the righteous few who were bound for heaven. Low self-confidence was actually sinful; it showed a lack of faith in God.

Anything other than your calling is a distraction. You have a purpose in life, the Puritans believed, and it is your bounden duty to pursue it. Any extras—fashions, seductive pleasures, even fancy speech—could pull you away from the single-minded pursuit of your calling.

This explains why the Puritans didn't set the world on fire with their fashions. Contrary to myth, they loved colorful clothing. But they knew that the vagaries of public opinion can yank you from your calling. Fashion complicates your life by seducing you into living the lives of others. It isn't a sin to be fashionable, the Puritans said, but fashion can lead you

---

Even Fewer in
England Could Have Done It

B OSTON BECAME INFAMOUS for its citizens' belief that their city was chosen by God and therefore superior to every other community on earth.
There is an old joke about an aged Bostonian who read Shakespeare for the
first time. "There are not twenty men in Boston who could have written
those plays," he said admiringly.

Moral: Confidence in self and place is not a sin, though it can get on other
people's nerves.

---

into sin. The Puritans' quest to avoid distraction became the essence of simplicity.

This book does not show you how to be a Puritan. Very few people
would want to be. Instead we will try to restore our forebears' canniest wisdom, the happiness that comes from living simply.

CHAPTER 3

Finding Your Calling

In which the reader is led through a personal biography
and begins acquiring some advantages of early New Englanders

MANY DESCENDANTS OF PURITANISM rejected the idea that some people were among the elect and the rest were doomed, but they still clung to faith in a person's calling. "Read your fate, see what is before you, and walk on into futurity," said Henry David Thoreau, who was no Puritan by a long shot.

If the notion of fate seems a little hokey in the twentieth century, take a look at your own calling—the unique set of skills and preferences that, properly understood, would head your life in the most desirable direction. Some things just come easily for you, while other forms of work or play seem like torture. You know you do best what you enjoy. The problem is, there's often too much white noise in your life—schedules, commitments, the vagaries of fashion—to let you determine your calling. Our lifestyles tend to fit our incomes and schedules (and then some), rather than our desires.

Have you noticed that some people don't appear to have this problem? They seem to be doing what they want to do. They don't look harried or pushed around, and some of them even have kids! And actually work for a living! Maybe there really is an elect, and maybe they're it.

Then again, maybe they're just lucky.

Consider the MacArthur "genius" fellows. The MacArthur Foundation is famous for its generous five-year grants to artists, scholars, journalists, and community organizers. The money frees its "fellows" from having to earn a living during the span of the grant. Anonymous judges choose the recipients in secret. You can't apply; the money just shows up, no strings attached. Newspaper reporters who tracked the lives of some of the genius fellows made a surprising discovery: Most of the recipients did what they were supposed to do. They wrote books, organized nonprofit groups, conducted research. Very few rented beach houses in the tropics and drank margaritas. For most MacArthur fellows, the money allowed them to do what they loved the most, which, for the most part, was what they were already doing. Is there any simpler life?

People who lead lives of good fortune tend to be extraordinarily skilled in going with their own flow. With unwavering dedication, courage, and ability, they commit themselves to what they want to do.

Luck, in short, comes most to those who know their callings.

RETIRE RIGHT NOW!
(The Catch: You Have to Keep On Working)

V ERY FEW PEOPLE get to be genius fellows, and that is a terrible shame. You may be a fellowless genius yourself. But there is an alternative that arises when people are sixty-five or so. They stop working and go on a permanent vacation called retirement. Most interesting about this group, however, is how few of them act like stereotypical golf-playing, sun-soaking, cruise-sailing retirees. The majority of people who retire do not go on what we would call a vacation. They work part-time, volunteer in their communities, run for public office, or continue their education. They often reveal their true callings for the first time in their lives. The sad thing is, most of us scheduled to retire in the next millennium will never retire in the traditional sense, according to the experts. We won't be able to afford it.

We may be doomed to live like Benjamin Franklin, who was eighty-one when he signed the U.S. Constitution.

Or like Paul Revere, who in his seventies began helping Robert Fulton make steam boilers that propelled boats and helped strengthen Boston's defenses in the War of 1812.

Or like John Kulish, who at eighty-five is a leading authority on the nature of southern New Hampshire. He can still carry a sixty-eight-pound canoe on his shoulders and hike all day without food and water. "I don't mind dying," he says. "I'm living on borrowed time as it is, but Jesus, how I'll miss the trout fishing."

Some people don't find their callings until they have "retired" from their careers. Other people do exactly what they want to do long before they're sixty-five, and then they just keep on doing it. Both groups have found their callings.

WHAT DETERMINES YOUR FATE

THE SIMPLE LIFE strays as little as possible from your calling, which in turn depends on three factors: what you have inherited, what happens to you by chance, and what you want.

You are stuck with your *inheritance*. This is the genetic makeup that gives you a prominent nose or overendowed rump. It is also the set of values and traditions you grew up with. Your inheritance is the life you have lived so far. We'll get to that in a moment.

Accident (and how you deal with it) is the second factor, such things as sickness, people you meet by chance, opportunities, catastrophes. You can prepare yourself for setbacks and moments of good fortune (this book will tell you how), but you can't count on them. Otherwise they wouldn't be accidents.

There is a third factor that can count as the most important of all, if you let it: your own *desires*.

If you can learn your calling from these three elements, you do more than simplify. You pursue happiness.

LOOKING BACK TO THE FUTURE

YOU CAN DISCOVER a lot about yourself by studying your inheritance. Your genes are visible to you every time you look in the mirror. First, though, let's talk about the part of your inheritance that is much less visible, your own past. "It is as hard to see one's self as to look backwards without turning round," Thoreau said.

To see yourself, you need to turn around and look backward.

One of the purest forms of your personality is your seven-year-old self. At the age of seven you have left babyhood and have acquired much of the personality you will be blessed, or stuck, with for the rest of your life. "Show me the boy of seven and I will show you the man" goes an old Jesuit saying, which works just as well with little girls. By the time we are seven our preferences are marked. Did you ask a lot of questions like a budding journalist, or have a passion for blocks like a carpenter or engineer, or prefer making up rules to the game itself (like a lawyer), or love the outdoors, or reading, or playing doctor? The child really is a parent to the adult; you are the living heir of your seven-year-old self.

But not the spitting image, of course. For one thing, your current self probably has front teeth. And you almost certainly have habits that would have been a scandal during childhood. But wouldn't it be great to return to the best parts of your seven-year-old state?

Imagine recapturing the simple, defining desires you had then, and consider everything else clutter.

One source of clutter is the praise and criticism we receive through life. While we hear a lot about the benefits of "positive reinforcement"—buttressing little egos with well-timed bits of praise—we don't often hear about its potential drawbacks. The world would have been spared many forgettable authors if their early attempts at creative writing had been accepted with a bit less enthusiasm. In his autobiography Benjamin Franklin recalls how as a young printer's apprentice he wrote two ballads that sold briskly. "This success flattered my vanity," he says. "But my father discouraged me by criticizing my performances and telling me verse-makers were generally beggars. Thus I escaped being a poet, and probably a bad one. . . ."

On the other hand, there is an old story about a psychology professor whose class conspired to use him as the subject of an experiment in positive reinforcement. During one lecture, unbeknownst to the prof, the students "reinforced" him each time he moved toward the classroom door. If he gestured or took a step that way, they would smile, laugh more loudly at his witticisms, look more attentive. If he went away from the door, they would frown, turn their gaze elsewhere, murmur among themselves, and look bored. By the end of the lecture the professor was speaking from halfway out in the hall, without even knowing it. And he was a *psychology* professor.

Beware of being damned through feinted praise.

Advantaged Childhoods

✦ Daniel Webster grew up on a hardscrabble New Hampshire farm. He suffered from childhood rickets, a vitamin D deficiency caused by malnutrition and lack of sun. The disease made his forehead protrude, giving him the prominent brow he was famous for later in life. It made him look brilliant, people said, even godlike.

✦ Back in the 1920s a gang of boys took to hanging out in front of Old Man Barry's place in North Cambridge, Massachusetts, much to the distress of Mr. Barry, who wasn't fond of loitering delinquents. One of the gang's most loyal members built on these friendships, made a great many more, and ended up as Speaker of the U.S. House of Representatives. "I'd rather be a lamppost on Barry's Corner than be with any of the people I've met from around the world," Tip O'Neill once said.

✦ Bostonian Amy Lowell suffered a glandular problem during adolescence and became unusually fat. Ostracized by children her age, she turned to poetry. Her first book, *A Dome of Many-Colored Glass,* published in 1912, established her as a literary powerhouse.

✦ Mary Baker was a sickly child, suffering from colds, fever, backache, lung and liver troubles, and, worst of all, dyspepsia. As an adult Mary Baker Eddy founded Christian Science.

✦ When P. T. Barnum was a four-year-old in rural Connecticut, his grandfather gave him his own farm, Ivy Island. At the age of ten his parents finally allowed him to see it. It turned out to be swampland. "The truth flashed upon me," he later wrote in his autobiography. "I had been the laughing-stock of the family and neighborhood for years." He went on, of course, to become one of the greatest hucksters in history.

+ When Clara Barton was twelve, she fainted at the sight of an ox being butchered. From then on she was a vegetarian. She lived to age ninety.
+ Richard Henry Dana suffered a serious ear injury when a schoolteacher yanked it. He grew up to be a lawyer whose court fights on behalf of sailors helped tone down the cruel discipline on American ships.

Moral: For some people, childhood difficulties turn out to be adult blessings.

EXPERIMENTING WITH YOUR FATE

To examine your past self and to learn more about your desires take a little experimentation.

Researchers know what the rest of us often don't consider: When you're studying something impossibly complicated, look at just part of it. Take, for example, two common items in a New England forest: chipmunks and trees. Any scientist will tell you that one of the worst ways to determine how many chipmunks there are in a forest is to try to count every one of them. Instead scientists will count just some of them within a small, plotted-out area and then make an educated guess about the whole forest. They call this a plot sample.

Trees are easier to count since they generally hold still better than chipmunks. But to examine an entire tree is trickier than studying a chipmunk. It is cumbersome to take a tree apart, and besides, it kills the tree. Instead researchers bore into the trunk and take out what is called a core sample. By examining the little cylinder of wood, they can tell the tree's age, its health, the types of nutrients in the soil, even the region's climate for as long as the tree has lived.

What have trees and chipmunks to do with your life? Nothing! Because of that, we miss a valuable technique for determining what you want. To simplify your life, you don't need to study your relationship with your parents or undergo psychoanalysis. You need only sample yourself, study the parts that can use simplifying, and record over a reasonably short period your habits and ways of doing things. So let's bore a bit into your life.

Don't think that you have to go through all the exercises below. Remember, simplicity means doing nothing to excess. You can tell something about yourself by the kinds of questions you picked. We'll get to that later. There is no real need to write down your answers either. (But you weren't going to, anyway, were you?) Later you'll "funnel" this self-examination into distinct likes and dislikes and eventually further narrow these preferences into a genuine calling.

CORE SAMPLE: YOUR BRAIN

D ON'T WORRY. We don't mean an actual core sample, and the process doesn't require a drill. This part is painless.

Take the Shower Test—that is, take a shower or bath. What do you think of when you're bathing? If you don't think of anything, bathe at a different time of day.

What good is the Shower Test? It is a time when your thoughts spill over from other times. Many of us spend our bathing moments fantasizing, thinking of ourselves as improved versions of ourselves—superheroes, legendary lovers. If you're one of these people, think of that improved version. You'll want to remember it for later in this book.

Fantasize some more. Imagine that a rich aunt died tomorrow and left you a million dollars after taxes. What would you spend the money on? How would your life change? Now ask yourself: Could you do these things without the million dollars?

PLOT SAMPLE: YOUR DESTINY

"WHAT A MAN THINKS OF HIMSELF, that it is which determines, or rather indicates, his fate." So said Henry David Thoreau, who, like his ancestors, was crazy about the subject of predestination. We can learn a lot about our callings—and even hints of our destiny—by following clues to our own personalities and pasts. Let's start by taking a sample of your calling, the life you would live if you had the means to live it. Answer these questions:

What is the best weekend you ever had? Can you think of one that is even better?

What was the best vacation you ever had? How old were you? Whom were you with? How long did it last? What were the parts that made it the best? How likely is it that you'll have another one that good? Why? What would have to change in your life so you could have that vacation again?

Have you ever had times when you *weren't* on vacation that you enjoyed better than any holiday? What made those times so great? Could you get them back?

These times have something in common: When you are simply enjoying yourself, you are living your own life the most purely. The biggest source of stress in our daily existence comes from duties and activities that stray from that true life. What if instead we got to do entirely what we wanted to do during the day? What if our time was our own?

If you could retire right now, what would you do? Would you really want to do it for a decade or more?

If every day were an hour longer, what would you do with the extra hour?

If every week were eight days, what would you do with the eighth day?

If every year had an extra two weeks, what would you do with them?

Imagine the ideal country home. Picture it in your mind: the house, outbuildings, surroundings, people. Where is the house? Near a lake? In the middle of a farm field? In the woods? On the coast of Maine? Is it an old house or a new one? Do you think you could ever live like that?

If you could be as old (or young) as you want, what would your age be? Why? What would you gain (or, in some wonderful cases, lose) if you were allowed to be that age? Could you gain some of the same advantages without being that age?

What relaxes you most? Music? Being with friends? Reading a book? Watching TV? A drink? Exercise? Putting your feet up and doing nothing whatsoever?

What do you do when you're waiting in line?

When you eat a piece of pie, do you turn it before putting your fork into it?

If you can find any meaning in the last question, that alone says a lot about you.

CORE SAMPLE: YOUR DNA

L ET'S TAKE A LOOK at the part of your inheritance that is your genes through these questions:

Were all four grandparents alive when you were old enough to be conscious of them? Or do you still have pictures of them? Describe the looks you inherited. Now think of personality traits that you received: hot-blooded or even-keeled? A quick study or a still, deep pond? Affectionate or somewhat steely?

Which grandparent is your favorite?

What kind of person would you be if you had inherited all the best traits of these four people?

Can you describe ancestors who mean the most to you? If you don't have ancestors, try making some up. (Why not? It's a free country.)

Who was your favorite relative as a child? Why? Do you have any of the same traits?

PLOT SAMPLE: YOUR TRADITIONS

O UR FAMILY'S PASTS can have at least as much effect on our personal values and habits as, say, the news media or our current friends. Ask yourself:

Do you know any family stories?

What were holidays like when you were growing up?

How did your relatives express their religious faith or their lack of it?

Why does your family eat the way it does?

Are there old sayings that your family was repeating before you were born? This leads irresistibly to these questions:

Can you imagine your own grandchildren repeating something you like to say? Or fondly remembering a holiday tradition? Or passing on a recipe? Or remembering an anecdote you wish to blazes was forgotten?

Can you picture a statue on a town common of an ancestor that looks exactly like you? What noble feats did that ancestor accomplish to earn the statue?

What family stories are the most memorable to you?

CORE SAMPLE: YOUR CHILDHOOD

F OR THE LAST EXERCISE in determining your inheritance, let's get to the child-is-father-to-the-man part. This may be the useful way to find out the life that is most simple for you.

What made you cry when you were seven? Physical pain? Frustration? Fear? The failure to get the toys you wanted? Loneliness?

Can you think of your happiest moments when you were the same age?

What was your favorite childhood book? What is your favorite movie as an adult? Can you think of anything the two have in common?

What was your favorite game when you were seven? Was it a sport? Chess? Dolls? Capture the flag? Torturing plastic soldiers?

What is your favorite game today? Is it related in any way to the games you liked best when you were seven?

What were your greatest fears when you were seven? Today?

What was your most embarrassing moment as a child? Have you ever told someone about it? How did you feel while telling it? Is it a funny story or painfully revealing?

What got you in the most trouble when you were a kid? What got you in the most trouble in the past two years? Any pattern here?

What punishment did you hate most as a kid?

What is your favorite story about yourself as a child?

Which teachers meant most to you?

Who were your heroes as a child? What were the characteristics you most admired?

Who was your favorite relative? Why?

Was there a kid your age you looked up to? What was it about your friend that you admired the most? Are you a little embarrassed to remember this? Why?

Get a picture of yourself as a child; you at the age of seven would be ideal. What do you see? What does the picture have to do with the adult holding it?

FUNNELING THE DATA

AT THE END OF THIS CHAPTER we'll compare your biography with a new, improved version. First, though, let's establish some basic tendencies that help bring that picture of yourself into focus.

ADVANTAGES

What are your greatest strengths?

Friends
Words
Leadership
Mechanical ability
Morals and beliefs, and standing up for them
Athletics
Ability to withstand pain
Patience
Other

WEAKNESSES

Which of these are you worst at?

Friends
Words
Leadership
Mechanical ability
Morals and beliefs, and standing up for them
Athletics
Ability to withstand pain
Patience
Other

Think again of your main weaknesses. As you do, consider each of the following questions:

Which ones could you improve on, so they aren't weaknesses anymore? Which single weakness is the most easily fixed?

Which ones could you live with without feeling much the worse for them?

Which ones are you just plain stuck with, just can't be helped?

RISK TAKING

How true are the following statements for you?

My biggest regrets in life come from my failing to take risks and seize opportunities.

I'm a little too willing to jump into new things and not settle on something long term.

Sure, it's easy for you to tell me how to improve my life. You don't have my problems.

Better safe than sorry.

When I travel, I'd rather stay in a chain motel than an untried bed-and-breakfast.

Which of the statements above is *most* true for you?

Several years ago a Dartmouth student named Emily Hill got caught in a blizzard while on a bus tour in the mountains of China. Being an experienced outdoorswoman and the only passenger who could speak Cantonese, Emily helped lead the others to safety without serious injury, except for some pretty severe cases of frostbite. Two weeks later Emily was gored by a rhinoceros while hiking through Nepal's Royal Chitwan Park. As you might have guessed, Emily is a hardy young woman, and she recovered quickly. Within a week Jane Pauley of the *Today* show was interviewing Emily in Nepal and her relieved parents in Kansas City over a satellite link.

Emily later said the most interesting thing about her crises was the totally different reaction among friends of her parents in Kansas City and her fellow Dartmouth students. "See what happens when you let your daughter wander abroad?" her parents' friends said. Meanwhile, back on campus students were saying, "Man, I wish I'd had such a great experience!" And that leads to these questions:

Which reaction would your own be closest to?

Could you ever see yourself in Emily's situation?

Daniel Webster's Father Thought He Was the Laziest Boy He Had Ever Seen

G ROWING UP ON A ROCKY FARM in New Hampshire, young Daniel would run off fishing at the earliest opportunity, leaving cows unmilked, stone walls unmended, gardens unweeded. As a U.S. senator he was notoriously lazy at committee work. Yet Webster produced a prodigious amount of correspondence, speeches, and unequaled legal argument. He was one of the most productive characters in American history.

Webster's secret: He knew what gave him energy and what drained it. Fishing gave him energy, and as soon as he could afford it, he bought a seaside farm in Massachusetts where he could fish whenever he had a vacation. Public speaking gave him energy, and he devoted enormous time to writing his greatest addresses. Argument gave him energy, and that was why he loved the law and sat enraptured whenever Senator Clay or Calhoun addressed the Senate.

Webster wasn't lazy. He was just choosy. We could do worse.

Moral: Pleasure has more stamina than duty.

What is the riskiest thing you have ever done? (Hint: It doesn't have to be physically dangerous. It could entail proposing a new idea, asking someone for a date, or speaking in front of a large crowd.) What exactly was at risk when you did it?

Suppose you are driving through your neighborhood when suddenly a car breaks down at the intersection in front of you. Traffic starts backing up behind you. What are you inclined to do first?

1. Talk to the driver and work out a plan.
2. Direct traffic.
3. Try to fix the broken car.
4. Go from car to car asking if one of them contains a mechanic.
5. Stay in your car until traffic can move again.

There are no right answers to these questions, except when you carry them out to their extremes. It is bad to be foolhardy. It is also bad to be controlled by your own fears. Between these extremes there is a lot of room for interpretation.

ENERGY SUPPLY

How true or false are the following statements for you?

Talking one-on-one with people makes me feel drained afterward, especially if we're disagreeing.

I feel a little charged up when I can check something off from a list of things I've had to do.

When I'm alone and concentrating on something—a memo, a plan, or a presentation—I feel as if I could work forever.

I'm at my best when I'm under pressure.

PRIDE

The early Puritans considered pride a sin, and the term "self-esteem" wasn't in their vocabulary. Pride is not a sin anymore. In a way that is too bad. Our forebears were taught to give God the credit for blessing them with any skill or attribute. If during a life of diligence and hard work they accomplished absolutely nothing and lived lives of poverty and misery, well, they didn't have themselves to blame. That's another luxury of the past most of us must do without. On the other hand, we can use our feelings of self-satisfaction as measures of the lives we most want to lead. Answer the following questions to see how dangerously humble you are:

What did you do over the past year that makes you proudest?

If a movie were to be made of your life, what would its title be?

List three things you did in the past that you're proudest of. What did you give up to achieve them? Were your achievements worth the sacrifice?

List the aspects of your life that make you proudest, in the following categories:

Family
Work
Athletics or physical activity
Crafts or hobbies
Community service
Romance
Friendship
Possessions and income
Other

DESIRES

Now we get to the crucial part of simple living: determining what you actually want to do.

Look at the pairs of opposites below and decide where you lie between each one. Take the pair "Company-Solitude." If you hang out with your friends every night and hate being alone, you should place yourself far over on the "Company" side. On the other hand, suppose you're pretty popular with your friends but like going on a solitary jog now and then. You might want to place yourself in the middle between "Company" and "Solitude." In the same way, place yourself somewhere in the continuum from "Noise" to "Silence," "Active" to "Sedentary," and so on.

Company	Solitude
Noise	Silence
Active	Sedentary
Responsibility	Independence
Caring	Dutiful
Variety	Sameness

Now think: What parts of your life are most important for you?

The respect of others
Family
Romance
Travel
The outdoors
Physical appearance
Friendships
Other

Think next: Which of those elements could most use improvement?
Ask yourself: Which of them is most easily improved?

And ask, finally: What would you be willing to give up to make the improvements?

- ✦ Time
- ✦ A quarter of your income
- ✦ A quarter of your family life

How much would you be willing to put at risk?

THE SUM TOTAL

H AVE YOU NOTICED how close you are to setting goals for yourself? Let's take a break from that and summarize all this reading you have been doing about yourself. In a bit you will describe your own "calling" as a basis for improvement.

Look at your favorite photo of yourself. Why do you like it? Has it flattered some part of you that you're proudest of? Has it nicely hidden some physical part you'd rather hide? Are you doing something you especially love? Are you with someone you love? Are you in a place that has special meaning for you? Does the picture represent a time of life that you remember fondly?

Describe yourself from these points of view:

1. Your lover
2. Your parents
3. Your kids
4. Your boss
5. Your employees
6. An attractive stranger

What makes you different from other people?

How are you like your astrological sign? How different?

Now look at the questions you chose *not* to answer. Why did you skip them? Did they simply look as if they would take too long, or are there questions in your life you'd just as soon avoid?

Just as important, which questions got the biggest reaction from you? Why? Were you surprised by any of your own responses?

Hang on to those thoughts. You may want to use them in a minute.

YOUR CALLING

IT IS NOW TIME TO DESCRIBE who you are and what you want as your calling. You have already collected data—taking the Shower Test, thinking about what you would do if you could retire immediately, listing your recent accomplishments, describing your seven-year-old self. Then you funneled the data, forming a picture of your strengths and weaknesses, the degree of risk you like to bear, what gets you charged up, what makes you proud, and what you most want.

Now it is time to translate this thinking into action. Think of yourself a year from now, as optimistically as you can. How does the picture change? Your calling might include:

Where you want to live
Whom you want to live with
What you want to do most of the day
What you want to do in your free time
What you would like to own
What you wish you looked like

Which of these changes is most important to you? Which are the least important? Which are the changes you can make most realistically, and which would be considerably more difficult? This just might be the time to pick up pen and paper. (You probably haven't so far, so stop complaining.) Draw yourself a chart that looks something like Mary's:

MARY'S PREFERENCES

CHANGE	DESIRABILITY	COST (TIME OR MONEY)	TIME IT WILL TAKE
Become noticed in my profession	Extremely high	High in time	Five years
Overcome my fear of public speaking	High	Low (but it sounds scary)	Two years
Create a home entertainment center	Moderate	High in money	Three years (to save the money)
Lose four pounds	High	Low (though I don't do diets well)	Four months
Learn Italian	Moderate to low, to be perfectly honest	High in time	Four years
Read good literature	High	High in time	Lifelong

Sometimes your preferences order themselves without your even trying. A change that is extremely desirable, involves little sacrifice of time or money, and can be accomplished quickly can take a high priority. As you can see from Mary's chart, however, the choices are usually not that easy. Still, some patterns emerge. Let's suppose Mary ranked the changes in order of the goals she wanted to start working on right away. She might list them in the following order, from "do immediately" to "put off until I win the lottery":

Overcome my fear of public speaking
Lose four pounds
Read good literature
Become noticed in my profession [she figures that overcoming her
fear of public speaking gets her started on this goal]

The Hermit Who Got a Job

FOR ELEVEN YEARS Nathaniel Hawthorne wrote alone in his room in Salem, Massachusetts, seeing nobody. Then he moved to Boston, worked for a publishing house, and directed a customshouse. He married and became U.S. consul to Liverpool.

Hawthorne took stock of himself. He decided he was shy, but he wasn't crazy.

Moral: If a tendency becomes an obsession, then it is too extreme to be simple.

Create a home entertainment center [she begins to have doubts about the importance of this goal]

Learn Italian [*sure* she will, when Naples freezes over]

Mary figures she probably will take a crack at the first three goals right away. This is reasonable, but it will take some serious discipline. She will need:

✦ Several ways to measure progress on each goal
✦ Short-term targets to help her maintain her motivation
✦ Extra time in her life, carved out from time-wasting habits she wants to break and from other daily activities she thinks she can quit
✦ Good habits—i.e., habits that help her meet her goals

All these constitute the next several chapters. Like Mary, you are learning your calling and improving your opportunities. Already you are beginning to act like a good Yankee.

CHAPTER 4

Attempting Fate

*In which the reader converts desires
into goals that last forever*

A T THIS POINT you may have many preferences but no solid goals. Fine. The next step is to convert the preferences into goals. As Thoreau said, "In the long run men hit only what they aim at."

A goal is a preference with an education. It's taking your desires and focusing them in a disciplined way. The Puritans knew about goals instinctively; their earthly duty was to take their circumstances and skills and make something of them. We can do the same thing.

The Puritans could look ahead and see heaven, a goal that could really get them motivated. Your own future might look less celestial. But there is a trick to setting goals: The more deeply attached they are to your calling, the more likely you are to achieve them.

IF YOU ARE WHAT YOU EAT, THEN DIET IS FATE

V ERMONT-BASED *Eating Well* magazine made an interesting discovery about how people deal with goals. It once asked readers to send in stories about weight loss regimens that actually succeeded. The editors found a remarkably consistent pattern in the letters that came in. Almost every successful dieter recalled a kind of epiphany, "a point at which they decided once and for all to lose weight permanently."

For women, this critical point was the realization that their bodies did not match their self-images. The typical female dieter had a confrontation with herself in the mirror and decided that the blob in the size twelve dress simply wasn't the woman she knew. For most of the men, it was a medical crisis, a doctor telling them to diet or die. (It appears that men have fewer epiphanies in front of mirrors.)

Both sexes succeeded in losing weight over the long term because they attached their lives to this lifelong goal—literally in the men's case, figuratively in the women's (pun intended). All this should explain why nearly all New Year's resolutions, and 95 percent of all diets, do not work: They are attached to a date, not to your life.

Such resolutions are not entirely useless, however. They can be useful data for setting bigger goals, ones that become permanent parts of your life.

Let's list some resolutions and see where they lead.

Lose five pounds.
Learn French.
Travel.
Make more money.
Find a spouse.

Move to the country.
Become a hermit.
Do more community work.
Drink less.
Become a rock star.

How would any of these resolutions simplify your life? They probably wouldn't. But they could lead to some changes—new habits, new uses of time—that add up to simplicity. To do that, we need to take a closer look at each resolution.

Lose five pounds: Why would you want to lose five pounds?

+ If it's part of a larger goal to be healthier, then let's look at that larger goal. By cutting fat out of the diet, exercising, and eating smaller portions at mealtime, you probably could lose five pounds or more. Then the five-pound resolution serves as an interim measurement.
+ If you want to lose five pounds pretty quickly to fit into a bathing suit on your Florida vacation, fine. Just don't feel guilty when you gain the weight back. This kind of short-term goal doesn't simplify your life because it doesn't change your habits. But who's to argue against it?
+ Suppose you find the extra fat makes you feel and look older. You may be backing into another goal: to make your body match your self-impression. The best way to keep weight off permanently is to see the slimmer version of yourself as your *real* self. But why stop there? You probably want to look at other ways to bring your outward appearance down to your age: dress, hair, activities, and the like. (See Chapter 13 for more on bodily control.)

Learn French: What larger goal is implied by this resolution? Are you an avid traveler? Are you an intellectual who wants to read great works in their original tongue? Or do you simply feel inadequate when you order in a French restaurant? (It might be simpler to avoid French restaurants or at least the ones with snooty waiters.) In any case the larger goal should be linked with your view of yourself.

Travel: If you know you like to travel, then the question is simply how to afford the time and money. You need to weigh your wanderlust against other, competing preferences—a comfortable retirement, for example, or a challenging (and time-consuming) job. If travel is a consuming passion, then it can help lead you to other goals, such as a career that requires a lot of travel, or one that gives you considerable time off.

Make more money: As you have already seen, daydreaming about money is a great way to define your dreams. What would you do if you made twice the money you're making now? How could you do those things without the extra money? A 1994 poll by Roper Starch Worldwide for *Worth* magazine asked people how much they would need to earn a year to fulfill their dreams. The average answer: $102,200. Given that this was three times Americans' average household income, the poll adds up to a lot of unconsummated dreams. On the other hand, could some of them be fulfilled without the dough?

"Earning more money" is not the best of goals, in other words. But it can lead to some great ones.

Find a spouse: This resolution can be especially thorny because it requires a consenting partner. The cost of failure is great, and the spouse hunter puts rather a lot of pressure on dates. Nonetheless, a wish to get married can help lead you to more controllable goal setting. If you're just lonely, maybe you should look for companions, not a spouse. In a bit we'll deal with ways to set *targets* for measuring goals and how you can judge your degree of satisfaction.

Move to the country: Again the trick is to examine why this is your dream and then to ask if you can accomplish the same goals without the move. If you want to be close to the land, if you love the idea of waking up in a freezing house and trying to get the woodstove going, if you live for the day you can walk out your back door and head up a mountain, and if all these things are worth the sacrifice in career and money and convenience, then maybe you should prepare to move to the country. But if what you mostly want is quiet, a safe school for your kids, and a neighborhood where people know your name, you should seriously consider the alternatives: private school, a friendly co-op building, a bridge club, a soundproof den. Decide what is most important to you: the land itself or what it offers you. If it's the land, go for the land. If it's other attractions, you probably don't need to move to the country.

Become a hermit: Go on, admit it. The thought has crossed your mind, especially on your way to your umpty-umpth meeting. This is another useful daydream. It also makes a great idea for a vacation: Try being a temporary hermit for, say, a two-week vacation. Consider a retreat in a meditation center or monastery. Rent a cottage in Vermont's remote Northeast Kingdom. If you're an experienced backpacker, go on a "vision" quest, hiking alone and thinking about your life. When you return to work, your coworkers suddenly seem delightfully amiable.

Do more community work: Look into your motives. Are they sheer altruism? Do you like people to see you as a good person? Is there a cause that you burn to join? Or does a particular kind of work attract you, look like fun, promise some good friends? Fill in your dream with details. "Do more community work" is a vague resolution. "Work in the downtown homeless shelter" makes for more useful daydreaming. This is a goal you can research, something you can build your schedule and habits around.

Drink less: Does a two-beers-at-dinner habit give you a paunch that you'd rather not have? Then the goal should have more to do with the paunch than with the beers. Cut out one drink a night, eat less dessert, and start exercising. On the other hand, if you find yourself losing control at parties, or risking your marriage with nightly visits to the neighborhood bar, or driving after you've had several drinks, or feeling compelled to have a stiff one or two at lunch, then the drinking itself is a problem and possibly an addiction. We'll talk more about bad habits and addictions in the next chapter.

Become a rock star: It doesn't matter that you will never in a million years negotiate "Stairway to Heaven" on an electric guitar. Imagine yourself onstage in front of a jillion adoring fourteen-year-olds, or hopping to London on your private jet, or saying something outrageous on a late-night talk show. If any of this appeals greatly, ask yourself (in case you need to be reminded): Could I get it without being a rock star?

A mediocre saxophone player decided he liked appearing in front of big crowds and speaking on talk shows and jetting around the world. His musical skills made it unlikely he would ever go platinum. Instead, Bill Clinton got elected president of the United States. Some of the same desires, different goal.

ALL THAT GLITTERS IS NOT A GOAL

YOU MIGHT WANT TO CONSIDER these four criteria to make sure your goal is a good one:

1. It should be achievable without a miracle or dumb luck. Deciding to win the lottery can make for a frustrating goal.

2. The idea of working toward your goal should get you excited or at least sound like fun. You are unlikely to say knowingly, "I think I'll torture myself for a few weeks and then quit after I lose my self-respect."

Make sure you're not saying that unconsciously. Your goal can be tough to meet, but if each step along the way sounds like an act of utter masochism, then you might think of a more attractive goal, one that fits you more closely.

3. The goal should be at the root of your desires. The best kind gets down to what is most basic about you. When you think of some way, large or small, that you want to change your life, ask: "Why do I want to do this?" Keep thinking, leading yourself from desire to desire, asking why? until you can answer: "I want to do this for its own sake. It will make me happier. It will match my vision of myself."

4. If your goal is basic enough, it should allow more than one measure for achieving it. Imagine for a moment that you're a forty-year-old weekend jogger with the notion of becoming a competitive age-group distance runner. You hardly dare admit it even to yourself, but your dream is to enter a marathon someday. In the meantime you set a yearlong goal to become a pretty good runner for your age. You decide that at the end of the year you should be able to run for an hour without stopping, you want to work up to four miles in less than forty minutes, you plan to enter one ten-kilometer race and finish it, and you hope to avoid hurting yourself.

A year later, after sticking fairly well to a three-runs-a-week schedule, you have several certifiable reasons to be proud of yourself. You can run for a whole hour. You are not quite down to a forty-minute four-miler, but you're making progress. You thrilled yourself by completing your first 10 K. And except for a little soreness in the Achilles tendon, you are injury free. Three out of four. Not too shabby.

Set interim targets to measure progress against your goal. Imagine, for example, that you want to learn to type so you can be more comfortable with computers. One of your measures of success is to be able to type fifty-five words per minute on a keyboard at the end of three months. Reasonable targets might include typing fifteen words per minute within two weeks, twenty-five within a month, forty-five within two months, and on up to fifty-five. (Other measures of typing success, such as accuracy and skill in composing letters, can be similarly targeted.)

The notion of multiple measurements can work in any other area of goal setting. Suppose your objective is to earn enough money to buy a little cabin in Maine. You tell yourself that in five years you want your income to be up 10 percent, not counting inflation. Or you hope to save forty thousand dollars over that period. Or you want to find a camp that costs a lot less than forty grand. Succeeding at any one of these measures could get you the camp in Maine.

Try this strategy in setting goals for work, for family life, for learning a new skill, for fixing up your house.

With most goals, the hardest part is knowing when to be satisfied. Targets help tell you when enough is enough. Some of the happiest people you meet have greatly simplified their lives by being skilled at contentment.

FOUR OF NEW ENGLAND'S
MOST CONTENTED PEOPLE . . .

NORMAN ROCKWELL, who talked the way he painted, once said: "I have the best of all possible worlds and the best of all possible lives." He added: "I do ordinary people in everyday situations, and that's about all I do."

Joseph H. Choate was once asked who he would prefer to be if he could not be himself. "Mrs. Choate's second husband," he answered. Mrs. Choate's opinion was not recorded.

"My greatest skill has been to want but little," bragged Henry David Thoreau. When he was still living in a shack on Walden Pond, he wrote: "I intend to build me a house which will surpass any on the main street in Concord in grandeur and luxury, as soon as it pleases me as much and will cost me no more than my present one."

Benjamin Franklin congratulated himself as an old man that he had only three fatal diseases.

... AND ONE OF THE LEAST

M ARK TWAIN WAS ONCE BANKRUPTED by his failure to know when enough was enough. In 1880 he invested in a typesetting machine invented by James W. Paige, an engineer at the Colt Arms Factory in Connecticut. Twain's original share was $2,000. He put in another $3,000 for improvements. A few years later Twain had invested a total of $13,000 when Paige told him that another $30,000 would easily finish the job. It was already the fastest automatic typesetter ever invented. Paige wanted to make it even better. By 1888 Twain was in for $80,000, but the machine was even more miraculous: It set type, adjusted the spacing, and even justified the margins, all automatically and at an unheard-of speed. But Paige thought it could stand some more improvements before it went on the market. He was still jazzing it up when the company went bankrupt. So did Twain, who was out $190,000. The typesetting machine was too complicated ever to work successfully, and Mark Twain spent the rest of his life writing and lecturing around the world, to pay off his creditors.

Contentment is a skill. It comes from setting the right targets and sticking to them.

USING ARTILLERY TO SATISFY

HOW DO YOU ACQUIRE the skill of satisfaction while avoiding Mark Twain's kind of mistake? It all comes down to target setting. We recommend the following technique, borrowed from the military.

Suppose you actually find a lovely little camp in central Maine. Sure, the cabin is falling off its rock foundation, the privy needs a new hole, the lake is small, and the place is on a little peninsula accessible only by water. The good news is, it's up for sale and you think you can talk the owner down to a mere $30,000. Now is the time to bring in the artillery.

No, we don't mean a city lawyer. The artillery is for you. Ever since people started throwing things at each other, they have been using two principles of gunnery.

The first is easy to understand: **The bigger the target, the easier it is to hit.**

The second principle is: **When you miss, consider it information, not a failure.** It works like this: When you lob at a target, aim at the target, but don't expect to hit it right away. Chances are you'll be a little short, or a little long, or a little to the left or right. If your shot falls short, aim longer next time. If the next shot is too long, place your aim between the first and the second shot. Artillery officers do not call this bad shooting, they call it bracketing. Medieval soldiers used it with catapults. Cannon crews used it in the Revolutionary War. You can use it for your own aims: to buy a camp in Maine, get in shape, or just organize your life.

Let's go back to the fishing camp. You're beginning to fall in love with that little broken-down place. But then you begin to suffer from the classic buyer's anxiety: What if the owner won't sell it to you for a low price? What if he sells it to someone else before you can raise the extra money? Now is the time to fall back on the two artillery principles. First, consider a bigger target, such as every appropriate camp for sale within a half-hour radius of the first one. If you bid on three places instead of one, you are more likely to have a bid accepted. "Target acquired," as they say in the military.

But suppose none of your bids is accepted. You still have principle number two to fall back on: A miss is a source of information. Maybe you're looking at the wrong area; research might reveal a more isolated part of Maine where camps are cheaper. Maybe you need to stop looking until you've saved more money. You could consider sharing the cost of a cabin with a friend. Or you might set your sights a little lower, buying a much cheaper camp without the waterfront.

Artillery Bracketing

WHEN YOU SET TARGETS to measure progress toward a goal, do what artillery officers do: Bracket your shots by aiming both high (your reasonable ideal) and low (the minimal effort you can get away with). Here are some examples:

Goal: To own a quiet retreat for relaxation and contemplation.
Target: Buy a camp in Maine.
High shot: A waterfront cabin that you buy within the year.
Low shot: A purchase price of thirty thousand dollars.
Range: You would be satisfied with a likable Maine cabin for thirty to forty thousand dollars within five years.
Plan: Search first for waterfront cabins in the thirty-thousand-dollar range.

(continued on next page)

Goal: To look as young as you think you are.
Target (along with finding a more flattering hairstyle and running three miles without collapsing): Lose weight permanently.
High shot: Lose five pounds in a month.
Low shot: Cut out one dessert a week.
Range: You would be satisfied to lose two to five pounds in six months.
Plan: If you don't lose any weight after cutting out one dessert a week for one month, start jogging and changing your diet.

Goal: To enjoy your work more.
Target: Find a good job.
High shot: Within four months, get offered a new job with more responsibility, more creative tasks, and flexible hours.
Low shot: Get new responsibilities at work.
Range: You would be satisfied to get new tasks within a year, at either your current job or a new one.
Plan: Update your résumé; start researching other jobs; put out feelers; talk to your boss about your future in the company.

You have not failed—yet—to reach your goal. You have simply shot too long (seeking too fancy a cabin for your budget) or too short (arming yourself with too small a budget). This is information, not failure.

It helps to bracket your target when you plan the goal. First aim high: What would be the best realistic outcome you could hope for? Then aim low: What would be the minimum you would be happy with? What would be the greatest cost you could bear? Then work for something in between.

Sometimes you will find yourself coming up with targets before you even devise a goal. That's fine; one of the easiest ways to establish a goal is to back into it, to discover it lurking behind a decision. Think about the major choices you have made in the past few years. Whether you regretted those decisions or not, the side you came down on tells something about yourself. That is what happened to Rebecca. She applied for a job and discovered a life's goal.

REBECCA CHARTS HERSELF

R EBECCA LIVES IN MASSACHUSETTS. Some years ago she worked as a supervisor in a small software company. She walked to the office and went home every day for lunch. She loved her work, but her career wasn't going anywhere. She wanted a bigger working environment, one where she could learn from other people and improve her technical skills. She applied and got an offer for a job at a large computer company in Boston, an hour's bus ride away. She was excited about the prospects, but she wasn't sure it was the right decision. So she made a chart.

If charting seems bothersome and un-Yankee-like, keep in mind that the Puritans were masters at the craft. Early New Englanders constantly set up tests for themselves, experiments to confirm their heavenly destination. Their diaries are full of checked-off lists. Benjamin Franklin took charting to an art form. At the age of twenty-two he decided to become morally perfect. "I wished to live without committing any fault at any time," he recalled as an old man. But, he wrote sadly, "I soon found I had undertaken a task of more difficulty than I had imagined." Taking a sheet of paper, he listed thirteen virtues, ranging from temperance to humility, and then put down a mark for every day of the week he violated one of them. "Chastity" ended up covered with the marks of failure. He never did master that one; one of his sons, born out of wedlock, became governor of New Jersey. "On the whole," said Franklin, "I never arrived at the perfection I had been so ambitious of obtaining." Still, he ended up "a better and a happier man than I otherwise should have been if I had not attempted it." He was not as easily discouraged as the rest of us mortals.

Rebecca, being no Franklin, created a much less ambitious chart. She was not after moral perfection, but the right job. To compare the benefits of each job she was considering, she assigned points on a scale from 1 to 5. Her chart looked like this:

SHOULD I ACCEPT THE OFFER?

BENEFIT	PRESENT JOB	OFFERED JOB
Career		
Prestige	2	4
Future employability	3	5
Mentors	1	4
Management skills	4	2
Enjoyment		
Nice office	4	3
Secretary	3	0
Travel	3	4
Independence	3	2
Daily challenge	3	5
Convenience		
Weekends free	0	5
Commute	5	1
Home for lunch	3	0
Flexible hours	5	3
Easy shopping	3	4

Note that Rebecca assigned only a "3" to "Home for lunch," even though this benefit applied only to her current job. She did this to assign less weight to lunch than she did to more important factors, such as "Commute" and "Flexible hours."

Now she added up the totals:

BENEFIT	PRESENT JOB	OFFERED JOB
Career	10	15
Enjoyment	16	14
Convenience	16	13
Total	42	42

"Well," Rebecca thought when she saw the totals, "*that* was a useless exercise." It was a dead heat. So much for the charting method of decision making. She considered flipping a coin—or, worse, calling her mother for advice.

But when she looked at the charts again, she found them more interesting. Her current job was probably more fun, and freer of hassles, than the other one would be. But the new job would clearly boost her career, and that was why she had applied in the first place. She thought about how she had given less weight to being home for lunch than she had to the commute. "Why don't I apply a weight to *each* of the benefits?" she asked. (Like many people faced with a big decision, she had begun talking to herself.)

Convenience was easily the least important benefit. Enjoyment was, oh, twice as important as convenience. And career? She thought hard and decided that given her long-term ambition, her career deserved twice the weight that daily enjoyment did. She scribbled these values on her chart and multiplied the "Career" totals by 4, "Enjoyment" by 2, and "Convenience" by 1. Her chart now looked like this:

BENEFIT	PRESENT JOB	OFFERED JOB
Career (x 4)	40	60
Enjoyment (x 2)	32	28
Convenience (x 1)	16	13
Total	88	101

The winner was perfectly clear. She took the new job and lived happily ever after.

Actually that's a lie. The commute turned out to be worse than she thought, and her new employers were reluctant to accept her ideas. She stayed less than two years and moved to western Massachusetts, where she started her own small software company.

Given the information she had at the time, she made a good choice. It just didn't turn out as well as she had hoped. The charts kept Rebecca from blaming herself. They also did something even more important: They allowed Rebecca to balance the importance of her career growth against other life goals, inspiring a series of thoughts that led to her starting her own company.

Decisions make some of the best mirrors. Rebecca's chart was better than any portrait. (She's a computer person. To her, a number is worth a thousand pictures.)

Rebecca has something in common with all the greatest New Englanders: *the sense that her goal is predestined.* "I realized, looking at those charts, that I was meant to be this ambitious," she says.

And that leads us back to one of our central morals: **A well-chosen goal looks a lot like fate.**

APPLYING YOURSELF

I T IS NOT ENOUGH to choose what you want and then assume that newly improved life will automatically follow. Like Rebecca, you should apply for it as well. We'll go through several steps to write résumés for life. Let's bring forward all the mental data you assembled in the previous chapter. If you are willing to commit yourself to one of the objectives you dreamed up, then you have already set yourself a goal.

Suppose it was to get a new job. What is the first thing you might do, especially if it were in an office? (Okay, what is the first thing you would do after you stopped imagining the things you would say to your current boss when you quit?) You probably would write a résumé.

This technique can work for noncareer goals as well. Suppose what you really want to do is lose weight and get in shape. Think up a résumé with which you "apply" for getting into shape. For "Objective," write: "To get less fat and stay that way." Below that, list your dieting and nutritional experience in the most positive way: the times you've lost weight; the exercise programs you have been through; the periods in your life when you looked the best; your greatest moments of self-control. (Again, it's not necessary to write the résumé down; just go over the objective and qualifications in your head.)

Sure, all the positive stuff you put in your résumé doesn't begin to give the whole picture. But remember, this is a résumé, not a signed confession. If you were applying for a job, would you feel compelled to reveal that you ate a crayon in kindergarten and got sick?

Winston Churchill had the right attitude. In his famous history of England, Churchill wrote magisterially about King Arthur, who may or may not actually have lived. "It is all true, or it ought to be," declared the statesman turned historian. Churchill would have written a heck of a résumé. He never let the facts get in the way of the truth. His declaration should

Job Résumé

Daniel Webster
c/o Office of the Secretary of State
The White House
Washington, D.C.

Objective
To be elected president of the United States

Experience
Secretary of state under three presidents
United States senator from Massachusetts
United States representative from Massachusetts
United States representative from New Hampshire
Practicing attorney

Accomplishments
Delivered more than four thousand speeches
Argued more than two hundred cases before the Supreme Court
Twice averted war with Great Britain
Opened diplomatic relations with Japan

Education
Read for the law in New Hampshire
Graduated from Dartmouth College near top of class

Fair health, married, enjoy hunting and fishing

References available upon request

Life Résumé

Daniel Webster
Marshfield
Massachusetts

Objective
To get rid of my nineteenth-century paunch and live long enough to be elected president of the United States
Experience
Was exposed early to involuntary dieting
Walked miles to school in New Hampshire climate
Showed stamina in delivering four thousand speeches, most lasting more than two hours
Accomplishments
Once took a trip without my portable bar
Have shown indomitable will with each goal
Walk every day into market for groceries

For reference you could talk to my first wife, but I outlived her.

be the motto of all introspective Yankees (unless he or she is writing a résumé that actually will be seen by a prospective employer, in which case the facts—the positive ones—are pretty important).

We're not just talking careers and dieting here, of course. Set as a goal the one part of your life that you most want to improve and that seems the most improvable: learning a language, getting your real estate license, doubling the time you spend with the kids, reading a good book every month, becoming a better lover, moving to some place you'd most want to live, learning to pray or meditate.

But this is not a diet book, or a time-management book, or a job-hunting book, or an enrich-your-relationship-discover-your-past-and-find-God book. This is a book about simplifying your life. To do that, you have already started thinking about your whole self and how you might gain control over it. You have thought about the advantages early New Englanders had and how you might acquire some of them yourself. You have started thinking about the choices you want to make. You may even have started making some of those choices, to move toward what you most want out of your life. Now let's figure out how to get those things for yourself.

CHAPTER 5

The Virtuous Weed

In which is revealed the simplifier's chief ally:
the obstacle in the way of a goal

IN 1622 A GROUP OF NEW COLONISTS arrived in Plymouth, Massachusetts, stretching an already limited food supply. Governor William Bradford wrote shamefacedly in his diary that the only meal he and the other hosts could provide was lobster. Today the critters go for as much as eight dollars a pound. Back in Bradford's time they would pile up onshore after a storm and stink the place up, causing major disposal problems. They were like weeds.

A weed, said Ralph Waldo Emerson, is a "plant whose virtues have not yet been discovered." Any gardener knows that a weed has its good points. If nothing else, it can tell what wants to grow on a plot. If left in the right place, it can help hold in moisture and soil. A good gardener doesn't merely throw a weed away; she uses it to her advantage.

Weeds of the Rich and Famous

✦ One hectic day in 1933 Ruth Wakefield, owner of the Toll House Inn in Whitman, Massachusetts, found herself too busy to melt chocolate for her butter dewdrop cookies. So she invented the chocolate chip cookie by accident. She cut large slabs of chocolate into pieces and dropped them into the batter, hoping they would melt in the oven. They didn't. Having no time to start over, she served them as "chocolate crunch cookies."

✦ Fifteen-year-old Chester Greenwood of Farmington, Maine, was missing all the fun. His friends were out skating on the town pond, and his parents had given him a brand-new pair of skates. But Chester's cold-sensitive ears kept him housebound by turning blue whenever he went outside. He got his mother to sew fur onto a doubly looped piece of wire, which he hooked on to a bowler hat, thus inventing the world's first earmuffs. He died a millionaire at the age of seventy-nine, having made Farmington the earmuff capital of the world.

✦ If a few riveters at the Fore River Shipyard in Quincy, Massachusetts, had been more honest, James J. Kilroy might have died a mere mortal. During World War II it was Kilroy's job to put a chalk mark next to every hole filled by the riveters, who were paid by the rivet. Some of them would erase the check marks to get paid twice. "One day," Kilroy's widow recalled when *Yankee*® magazine interviewed her in 1970, "just before he was going off duty, Jim heard his foreman ask one of these dishonest riveters if Kilroy had been there. When the man said no, my husband was furious, because he knew he'd already chalked that man's rivets. So he took his chalk and wrote 'KILROY WAS HERE' in letters too large and too bold to erase." From then on he wrote "Kilroy Was Here" next to every rivet. The ships went to sea bearing Kilroy's name all over the place. And "Kilroy Was Here" became a motto for the worldwide presence of the American military.

✦ When Fannie Farmer was a teenager in Medford, Massachusetts, she became seriously ill and was disabled for life. She turned to cooking and made it a science, encouraging accurate measurement and quality control. The *Fannie Farmer Cookbook,* first published in 1896 as *The Boston Cooking-School Cook Book,* couldn't find a publisher until Farmer offered to pay for the printing herself. The book became one of the greatest best-sellers of all time and is still in print.

✦ In 1876 Dr. Augustin Thompson of Lowell, Massachusetts, concocted Moxie Nerve Food to relieve "paralysis, softening of the brain, and insanity," along with "brain and nervous exhaustion, loss of manhood, imbecility and helplessness." The stuff sold pretty well. Thompson then created Beverage Moxie Nerve Food by adding soda water. The problem was, Beverage Moxie tasted terrible. So Thompson employed an old belief of New Englanders: If you don't enjoy it, it must be good for you. He dressed a respectable-looking man in a physician's white coat and had him urge people to "learn to drink Moxie." Throughout the twenties the beverage outsold Coca-Cola as America's favorite soft drink. You can still buy it in parts of New England.

✦ The man who inspired the Jules Verne novel *The Tour of the World in Eighty Days* was a Bostonian promoter named George Francis "Express" Train. In 1870 he went on a global tour to publicize completion of the Union Pacific Railroad. His trip actually took him eighty days plus one month (he spent the month in Paris helping out the Communards). Train

(continued on next page)

went on to beat his own record twice more. He also took time to be a successful businessman, builder of English street railways, radical advocate of women's suffrage, and candidate for president of the United States. His politics got him thrown into fifteen jails during his lifetime. "I have used prisons well," he said. "They have been schools to me, where I have reflected, and learned more about myself . . . and from them have launched many of my most startling and useful projects and innovations."

+ L. L. Bean's first Maine hunting shoes were duds. The stitching came out of the rubber bottoms, causing them to separate from the leather tops. Bean earned lasting mail-order fame by returning every cent of the first order, a loss of $350. "Nobody ever won an argument with a customer," he said. That adage became the central wisdom of one of the most successful catalog businesses in history.

Moral: If you're lucky, you too can be blessed with a worthy obstacle.

HELPFUL OBSTACLES

THE BARRIERS THAT STAND IN THE WAY of your desires—your personal handicaps, your fears, your repeated failures, external factors, the odds against you—all have their uses:

+ As information about yourself and your goal
+ As pathfinders to help you fine-tune your life's direction
+ As the very means of achieving your goal

And on top of all the other benefits:
+ As a great way to lower other people's expectations

Let's start with the expectations-lowering part since that's the easiest. (One tenet of simplicity is to do first what is easy.)

You might want to share your goals with other people; the risk of embarrassment can be a great motivator. Or your goal may have been set in part by another person, such as a boss. In any case, set public expectations as low as possible; then exceed them as much as you can. Well-run hotels use this principle. Call room service, and it will tell you that your meal will come "in twenty to thirty minutes." But it intends to deliver within fifteen to twenty minutes. If it meets its own target, you're pleasantly surprised. If it misses, it's still on the schedule it gave you. Similarly, a good catalog company will set a generous deadline when it estimates delivery of your package. When you lower expectations, you cut yourself some slack. When you exceed expectations, you look like a hero. That is the wonderful thing about the obstacles that you face on your way to a goal. You're usually better off when you overcome them than if the obstacles were never there.

HOW TO CLASSIFY AN OBSTACLE

OBSTACLES CAN ALSO OFFER some important data for your own purposes. But you have to know how to read them. We mentioned earlier the most common barriers to accomplishing a goal:

- ✦ Personal handicaps (including fear or a lack of motivation on your part)
- ✦ External factors
- ✦ The odds against success
- ✦ Your own failed attempts to meet the goal

You have four choices with each type of obstacle: You can back down from your goal (this isn't necessarily a bad thing, as you shall see). You can overcome the obstacle somehow. You can figure out a way around it. Or you can use it as a means toward your goal. To make your choice, you should examine your obstacles closely. Are they permanent barriers? Will they go away by themselves if you wait a bit? If you can overcome them, will you succeed? Is the goal worth the effort?

High People with Low Expectations

◆ Paul Revere's first newspaper ad in the Boston *Gazette*, September 19, 1768, offered custom false teeth. Revere wrote that they looked natural and allowed "Speaking to all Intents." He did not claim that you could chew with them.

◆ Newspaper editor Horace Greeley was once asked what he called a successful lecture. "When more folks stay in than go out," Greeley replied.

◆ The New England Patriots had a long tradition of losing football games, but they were especially bad when Bill Parcells took over as coach in 1993. During his first year with the team it still had a losing season, but fans were thrilled that it had a few wins. The next year the Patriots actually made it to the play-offs. They got knocked off in the first game. Did New Englanders lament their lost hopes for the Super Bowl? Not on your life! They declared Parcells the best coach in the history of the world. In two short seasons he had taken the team from the cellar to, well, pretty high.

Moral: In lowering expectations, you turn disadvantages into advantages.

For illustration, let's consider Mary, who listed her preferences at the end of Chapter 3. She has chosen three goals that could in various ways simplify her life: to overcome her fear of public speaking, to lose four pounds (and keep them off), and to read good literature. She listed other preferences but decided that she shouldn't complicate her life by attempting to simplify to excess.

Before we get to the obstacles, we should ask how her goals lead to simple living. Wouldn't the effort count as a lot of extra bother? Mary's answer is that these goals should help *eliminate* some of the bother. She is rising in the advertising profession but finds that her terror of speaking in front of people is holding her back. She wants to lose some weight because she is tired of seeing a slightly misshapen person in the mirror. The Mary who steps out of the shower in the morning is not the Mary she knows; that's complication enough for her. Finally, she wouldn't admit this to anybody, but one of her motives for reading literature is pretty close to the one for losing weight: She finds herself a little less interesting when alone with her thoughts than she used to be and fears that the Mary she loves is becoming a bit shallow.

She lists the obstacles in the way of each goal:

Public speaking. Lack of motivation and time are the biggest barriers. She looks into acting lessons, considers hiring a speech coach, calls the local Toastmasters club. These alternatives gall her; she just can't see herself doing any of them. She prices some video cameras, thinking she might try taping herself in private. But she never gets around to buying one.

It occurs to Mary that she just doesn't see herself as a public speaker and that she should consider other ways of advancing herself professionally. She decides to compromise, agreeing to lead small meetings in the hope that she'll get used to it. She also buys herself a pocket tape recorder and starts dictating her letters. The practice can't hurt, she figures.

Will all this eliminate her fear? Probably not, but then, Mary is pretty sure she will always be anxious in front of a crowd. She can't eliminate that obstacle; she can just reduce it a bit. Should she feel like a weenie for failing to tackle the problem head-on? Not unless she enjoys belittling herself. Besides, she has learned something about herself, not a bad goal in its own right.

Losing weight. Here Mary knows exactly what the obstacle is. She adores chocolate. When she was younger, her body processed the fat and sugar pretty well, and she could maintain a reasonable weight even while eating chocolates in front of the TV every night. Since she turned thirty, she finds that her thighs are not quite so forgiving. If she can ditch the candy, she can respect herself in the mirror. But Mary just can't imagine a life without chocolate. So again she compromises. She limits her candy eating to the weekend, changes her television-watching habits to avoid temptation, and buys an exercise video for a ten-minute leg routine every morning.

This discipline becomes habit for Mary after a few months, and her thighs show their appreciation. This is not to say that she unfailingly keeps herself from weekday chocolate binges. Mary is no saint. But occasional lapses do not prevent her from her goal of losing weight; they just delay it a bit.

Reading. The biggest obstacle here is time. Mary decides to cut out half an hour of television before bed and spend the time reading. (This happens also to be when her craving for chocolate is strongest.) Occasionally, when she just doesn't feel like reading, she keeps the television on. But more and more she finds it difficult to fall asleep without a half hour or so of quietly turning pages.

Moral: The most achievable goals bring you back to yourself.

Mary's goals for losing weight and reading became natural appendages or parts of her life. Her public-speaking goal comes harder because she doesn't see herself as being a speaker. It's an appendage that does not attach easily.

Maybe it never will. But there is a technique Mary could use to try to change that mute impression of herself. It entails getting her head into training.

THE MIND BARRIER

As MARY'S EXAMPLE SHOWS, one of the most intractable barriers to achieving a goal is the failure to believe you're capable. The Puritans saw self-doubt as a temptation of the devil. A lack of confidence showed a lack of faith, a sign that a soul was hell-bound.

Athletes leap the mind barrier with a skill called visualizing, a way of learning to believe in yourself. Olympians have proved its effectiveness. You can get into the habit of visualizing to attach yourself to your own goals.

One of the world's best visualizers is John "Morty" Morton, a former Olympic biathlon competitor and coach. When he was in his late forties, Morty decided to become the nation's top cross-country skier for his age. He spent a year working on his goal, and he met it. Morty quit his job and used his savings to compete all over the United States and even Europe. When he was done, he wrote a book, appropriately titled *Don't Look Back*, to advise and inspire other middle-aged athletes. Now in his sixth decade, he looks thirty, tops. He runs up mountains better than most college-age athletes. Yet he seems like a pretty laid-back guy. Maybe this attitude comes from the big sauna he built himself, heated with wood he cuts from his own trees in Thetford, Vermont. But a lot of his youthfulness is in his head. Morty visualizes young.

Visualization is nothing more than the disciplined imagination of success. A downhill skier stands at the top of a slope, eyes closed, skiing the course in her mind. A runner imagines the gun going off again and again and each time pictures himself breaking the tape ahead of everyone else. "The mind holds the key to achievements far beyond the generally accepted level," says Morty, who ought to know.

Visualizing is pretty simple, but that doesn't make it easy. Morty says it takes practice and mental conditioning, the way a sport takes physical training. Here are some tips, most of them interpreted from his book and applied to simple living.

- ✦ **It's hard (on you) to be humble.** If we do something well, we should be the first to admit it to ourselves—though not necessarily to others, of course. Yankees hate to brag—at least of themselves.
- ✦ **It's good to think about the future, so long as that future seems bright.** "For most of us it seems easier to imagine the worst-case scenario than the best case," Morty says. He attributes this trait to the Puritan ethic, but as we have seen, we shouldn't blame the Puritans. They imagined a worst-case scenario for everybody else, while keeping optimism to themselves. Not a bad strategy.
- ✦ **Turn obstacles into stepping-stones.** What seem to be disadvantages to some people are advantages to others. When it rains before a ski race, Morty looks up cheerfully and says, "Good! I'm a mudder!"

    A pessimist acquires a self-centered boss and curses her fate. A visualizer thinks, "I know how to handle egotists," and imagines herself using this new supervisor as leverage to get herself promoted up and out of the department.

+ **Forgive yourself any temporary failure.** The Puritans saw their mistakes as exceptions that proved the rule, as we shall soon see. Follow their example.

+ **Constantly imagine yourself having met your goal.** Do you want to get a night school business degree? Picture yourself, in detail, devising market strategies for your employer, using your hard-earned knowledge long before you've actually earned it. Do you want a different job? Picture yourself in it. Morty says to use all your senses. Smell the carpet; hear the sound of the laser printer ejecting your latest spreadsheet; see your mahogany desk; feel the expensive flannel of your suit. You can picture yourself internally, looking out at your new improved world, or externally, as if watching yourself in a videotape. Try it both ways, though Morty claims the internal version gets better results.

+ **Attach yourself to someone who seems a little better.** Morty would "lock on" to a racer who passed him, hanging on to this faster racer's pace and looking for an opportunity to repass. We can do this outside sports. As Chapter 8 shows, the people we lock on to are called mentors.

+ **On the other hand, don't get fixated on the competition.** Morty imagines himself as an artist in front of an empty canvas. Every race is an opportunity to paint a masterpiece. "What any other artists do is totally irrelevant," he says. "The canvas I face is mine alone." What a great way to see a goal: as a work of art.

John Morton links this thinking habit with his goal of becoming a top age-group athlete. If you set the right goals, habits can take you a long way toward them, without much thought, and that, after all, is the whole point of a habit.

Noble Failures

✦ Benjamin Franklin's famous kite experiment does not seem to have done him any harm. But he nearly killed himself trying to execute the Christmas turkey. He was holding both electrical wires in one hand when he touched a piece of metal, unwittingly turning himself into a conductor. After a flash and an explosion Franklin went into convulsions. No one knows what happened to the turkey. The inventor continued his electrical experiments after he recovered.

✦ When John Ledyard dropped out of Dartmouth College in 1773, he returned home to Connecticut by hollowing out a tree log and paddling this homemade canoe down the Connecticut River. Impressed into the British Navy, he sailed with Captain James Cook to Hawaii and watched the indignant islanders butcher the explorer. In 1785, during a visit to Paris, he met American Ambassador to France Thomas Jefferson. Eighteen years before the Lewis and Clark Expedition, Jefferson supported Ledyard's idea on how to explore the American West. The plan was to travel across Europe and Russia, sail to the American west coast, and trek eastward. Ledyard got to within some five hundred miles of Russia's Pacific coast before Empress Catherine, thinking him a spy, had him arrested and dumped on the Polish border. Ledyard ended up that same year in Cairo planning to explore the African interior. While taking an emetic to soothe his nerves—it had been a rough year—he vomited so violently that he burst a blood vessel and died on the spot. Jefferson wrote later, "Thus failed the first attempt to explore the western part of our Northern continent." Nonetheless, in all his failure to finish anything, Ledyard managed to explore on foot more land than anyone else of his century.

➤ Charles Goodyear was perpetually in debt and spent much of his time as a young man in debtors' prison. Then he heard that rubber manufacturers were suffering from their material's propensity to melt in hot weather. He could make a fortune if he could find a means of vulcanizing rubber—making it stronger and more flexible. His home in New Haven stank with the smell of cooked rubber. When he went to debtors' prison, he continued his experiments there. Then, in 1839, he was boiling rubber and sulfur on his brother-in-law's stove in Woburn, Massachusetts, when he dropped some of the stuff on the stove. The cooled rubber was—shazam!—vulcanized. It took him five years to get a patent, but by then his process was being pirated all over the place. In 1852 Goodyear fought a court battle in New Jersey, represented by Secretary of State Daniel Webster, who won the case but charged a fortune for the effort. When Goodyear died in 1860, he was two hundred thousand dollars in debt.

➤ Richard Jordan Gatling of Hartford, Connecticut, was the son of a North Carolina inventor. In 1861, obsessed with the notion that a hugely destructive machine could be horrible enough to end all wars, he designed a gun with eight to ten barrels that revolved on an axis. The Gatling gun worked beautifully, except in its original peaceful purpose. Gatling went on to invent a tool that was more overtly peaceful, a motorized plow.

Moral: Some of the most accomplished people are those with the courage to fail.

ON SINNING AND FORGIVENESS

There are two basic problems with setting goals:

1. You might fail to meet them.
2. You might meet them.

The trouble with meeting a goal is the temptation to go on permanent vacation, to lose the incentive that the goal gave you in the first place. Suppose you "acquired" a target of losing five pounds. You already look younger! You've met your goal! You reward yourself with a chocolate cake and forget about dieting. Don't mistake a target—a temporary measure of progress—for a long-term goal. Losing five pounds is not the same as becoming permanently thin. The best goals are permanent ones.

Missing your targets, on the other hand, might not be such a bad thing. Suppose that instead of losing weight over a month, you gained it. You're going in the wrong direction! You're a sinner, headed for diet hell! One hot fudge sundae, and you've blown your diet. An evening in front of the television, and you've lost your plan to read a dozen books a year. A night out bowling is a betrayal of your resolution to learn a foreign language, or rewrite your résumé, or volunteer at a soup kitchen. We see these little side steps from our goals as permanent, irretrievable sins, proof of our inescapable fallibility. You curse the Puritans for burdening your culture with so much guilt.

But should you be blaming the Puritans? They believed you couldn't earn your way to heaven. Your behavior on earth was just an outward indication of whether you were destined for heaven or hell. If you were venal or lazy, that was the way God made you; you were one of the unfortunates doomed to inherit Adam's original sin. If, on the other hand, you were thrifty, honest, and hardworking, you were clearly one of the elect, one of God's chosen even before birth.

Needless to say, this belief made for some nervous moments on deathbeds. On the other hand, a Puritan who was convinced he was one of the elect didn't have to worry about straying from his goals. He plodded sturdily (if in something less than a straight line) toward sainthood because his success was predetermined. Who was he to second-guess his Maker? You would think this made Puritans a pretty somber lot, constantly checking to see if their moral flies were open. This is in fact the case. Still, their diaries show they could tell a joke, and to judge from records of alcohol consumption, they didn't hold back at a party. The Puritans knew how to sin properly. A little petty straying didn't mean you weren't perfect, for a human. This may be inconsistent philosophy, but it was wise living.

Contrast this attitude with our own. We slip a little in our pursuit of goals and think we're doomed from ever meeting them. If only we could be as forgiving about it as the Puritans!

We also have to believe ourselves capable of meeting our goals. This makes us able to allow a small detour now and then. So what if you gained weight in the first month of a diet plan? You've missed the target, not the goal. A month is a short stretch of your life. Maybe your plan was unrealistic. Maybe it will take different habits, less food, more exercise. Maybe you haven't yet made your goal an appendage of your life. Maybe you're not *supposed* to weigh that little. That missed target is valuable information, not eternal damnation.

CHAPTER 6

Lodes of Time

Regarding an unearthed treasure of simplicity: the ill-used hour

IT IS ALL WELL AND GOOD to talk about mental attitude, but even the most positive frame of mind isn't going to give you time off from your job or do the shopping while you pursue a simpler life. Remember the question asked in Chapter 3: What would you do if you had an extra hour in the day, or day in the week, or week in the year? That may sound impossible, but windfalls do come occasionally. Have you ever come across some unexpected cash while cleaning the house? Wouldn't it be great if you could find time in the same way? Actually you can. You just need to do some weeding, to root out pockets of time.

One such time pocket arises out of our own good nature. Much of our day-to-day clutter—a frantic schedule here, a small conflict there—comes from our having said yes too many times. We tend to take on time-eating social and family obligations as they come, without considering them

Nostalgia the Way It Used to Be

✦ Bostonian Ruth Stout became famous when she published her book, *Gardening Without Work,* while she was in her seventies. She practiced what she preached, which wasn't just gardening. She ordered supplies by mail and froze vegetables to get her through the winter. When she was ninety-five, she bragged that she hadn't visited a supermarket in fifteen years.

✦ You might say that Yankees invented fast food. One of the simplest meals in America is classically Yankee in origin and spirit: the New England boiled dinner, which you make by throwing a meal into a pot. The chief original ingredient was beef preserved by a long soaking in a brine of salt and gunpowder. In those days most people kept their gunpowder in cornucopia-shaped containers called corns. Hence "corned beef." You can make the dish today. Take a brisket of corned beef (gunpowder is no longer an ingredient, so the meat doesn't have quite the same zing). Boil it with potatoes and vegetables, stud the meat with cloves, and glaze it with maple syrup. Most people wouldn't find it the best-tasting food in the world, but it's easy to make and filling.

Moral: Saving time is a matter of weeding.

all together. If we're asked to serve on a committee or help organize a fundraiser, we do it. If our kids want to join a team, or take more lessons, or do anything else to add to our chauffeur's duties, we say okay.

We need to know how to make the big decisions that allow us to avoid the little ones. If you refuse your kids ballet on top of piano and soccer, will they grow up to write nasty books about your parenting? Do you really have to sell raffle tickets for the volunteer fire brigade, or is it enough that you serve on the PTA and organize the annual neighborhood food drive? Your willingness to say yes makes other people ask you all the more. And you're beginning to think you're something less than a saint; you're a sucker. You need to learn the noble art of saying no. This art consists of several techniques.

First, **list your functions.** Consider ranking your philanthropic activities. Agree to a temporary assignment more readily than a long-term assignment. Put family before community. Give priority to activities and causes that you genuinely enjoy and that give you energy.

Once you have rated this outside-the-home, nonpaying work, **give yourself a limit** to the number of activities or the amount of weekly hours devoted to them. Apply this principle to children by limiting them to, say, one sport and one other regular activity at a time. If a kid is dying to join the Scouts, first she has to give up weekend soccer.

If nothing else, a keen knowledge of the time you and your family spend, and how much you have to spend, can give you something to say when the call comes asking you to serve on another neighborhood committee. "Gee, I'd like nothing better," you can say with all sincerity, "but I'm booked solid for the next six months. I'd appreciate your considering me if a slot opens up next spring. By then the basketball league should be winding down."

This telephone technique leads to another suggestion: **Never say yes right away.** If the request for your time is not an emergency, ask for a day or two to think about it. Find out how much time it will take, and balance it against the time you have to spare. Consider your qualifications for the work, even if the duties do not seem terribly significant. Are you the best person for the job or simply the most available?

Ask yourself: What's the pay? Of course there isn't any of the monetary kind; that is the very definition of volunteer work. But to use your time wisely and to put your heart into the task, there should be some other compensation. Who benefits from your work? Are you enjoying it personally? What are you learning? What part of your life, or which member of your family, will benefit?

Have an arsenal of noes. Many times we say yes simply because we don't have a no ready. It's hard to turn something down, especially if we feel flattered that someone thought to ask us in the first place. Often the person on the other end of the phone is a volunteer herself, and the favor she asks can seem like a personal one. You need to have something to say. Try keeping little scripts by the phone: "Wow, [first name], I would really love to do that, but I'm right in the thick of [seasonal or temporary activity] and I just couldn't do justice to [request]. But I really appreciate your thinking of me, and if you need me for anything toward the [next season], I hope you think of me again."

This script doesn't burn any bridges. It makes you seem like a willing, friendly person, even while you're turning the job down. On the other hand, if you want to kill the request dead, you need more permanent-sounding language, like "Gee [first name], I wish I could, but I just don't see how I could give [request] enough time to do it justice." If you can volunteer another name without feeling guilty about it, this is a good time to do it.

DIGGING UP THE COUCH POTATO

THE ART OF SAYING NO is crucial for preventing additional duties from crowding out your life. But the biggest potential pockets of free time are actually *wasted* time: television, early morning, and the hours when you are on the move. Like Emerson's virtuous weeds, they can be put to good use.

Television may make the single biggest difference between family life today and as it existed in early New England. That may explain how people managed to be so productive. The average American family keeps at least one TV set on for more than seven hours every day. This doesn't mean that every member stares silent and slack-jawed at the screen the whole time. For many households the TV acts as a kind of picture window to the world outside. Family members talk, eat dinner, do their chores in front of the television, glancing now and then if something attracts them. This can't be great for sustained conversation, but it is not necessarily bad living.

Even if you do tend to sit mindlessly in front of the tube, maybe that is exactly what you want. You're tired after a hard day's work; you don't care to think for a while.

> # Channel Surfing and Eternity
>
> ———❧———
>
> "**A**S IF YOU COULD KILL TIME without injuring eternity," said Henry David Thoreau.
>
> **Moral**: Think what Thoreau would have said about television.

Or you switch on the public station and passively absorb some culture and science. Nothing wrong with that.

But if your TV watching is a regrettable habit, well, that's a good thing, too. It's a rich source of time that with a little effort you can convert into an extra daily hour or so.

Excess complicates your life. Anything done in excess offers an opportunity to simplify your life. Not that you have to throw out your television. That solution might be excessive and therefore not simple. Think of the ways you most want to improve your life, and the time you would like to have every day and every week to improve it. Then decide the best course to take with your TV watching. Some choices:

1. Keep the TV on as much as before. Just schedule your watching time so that you do other activities simultaneously. Here are some examples of what you might do in front of the tube:

✦ If one of your goals is to get fitter, try exercising or stretching, or both, while you watch television. Plan a routine around four of your favorite half-hour shows every week, so that the shows are linked to your exercise. This alone frees two hours of precious personal time weekly, without your having to give up any TV watching.

✦ If exercise isn't what you have in mind, try such crafts as knitting or rug hooking. Use television time to make gifts for family and friends. For some people, TV seems more pleasurable when they're making something in front of it. It seems a bit like a fireplace that way.

✦ Suppose you plan to give your family better meals, or you want to improve as a cook. Schedule a new recipe every week, and make it in front of an early-evening show. (Obviously it helps to have a TV set in your kitchen.) Try preparing meals that can be served the following day; this way you can schedule fancy-cooking time around your favorite shows.

✦ You can greatly raise the quality of your TV watching, and cut out the commercials, with a little advance planning. If you have a videocassette recorder, spend an hour or two with a notebook in a video rental store and write down all the movies you want to see in the next several months. If you get cable television, program the VCR to record the movies on your list. Or rent them, checking off the ones you see. (A list saves a lot of time in a store.) Good video catalogs allow you to make your list without leaving home. Try "The Video Catalogue" (1-800-733-2232), "Critics' Choice Video" (1-800-544-9852), or "Time Warner Viewer's Edge" (1-800-224-9944). An alternative to cable and rental is a friend with a video collection.

Ask coworkers and neighbors if you can borrow or swap tapes on your list. Public libraries lend videos for free.

2. Keep watching TV every night but cut back an hour. If you average two hours nightly, try just one hour. Spend that other hour on your goals. Here are a few ways you can use the extra time:

✦ Go to bed an hour earlier. Why? See the section below on the benefits of getting up early.

✦ Read books. Suppose you read a paperback at the rate of twenty pages per hour. If you switched an hour's TV time to books every weeknight, you could read a dozen a year. Schedule this reading time for the hour before you go to sleep, and do it in bed. After a couple of months you might find that you can't go to sleep without reading. Congratulations, you have acquired a new habit—one that enlightens rather than tranquilizes.

✦ Write letters; call friends.

✦ Do volunteer work.

✦ Study for a night course.

✦ Do some outdoor exercise like jogging.

✦ Schedule family time. If you have kids, set the time for the end of homework (a good incentive to get it done). Play video games on the TV, or Ping-Pong in the basement, or cards. Your family may balk at time away from television. Commit them to a month of this new routine. Do things that the other members want to do even if they give you a headache or bore you to tears. Make the time a family habit.

3. Put the television in an inaccessible part of the house, or keep it in a closet. Is there a guest room you usually keep unheated? That's the perfect place for a TV. Heat the room on the special occasions you want to watch something. Keep just one set in the house, and produce it only when the reason to watch it outweighs any other use of your time. At the very least, remove the television from your bedroom. When you are tired, you can fall prey to temptation.

4. Toss the TV. This is an extreme measure; it's up to you to determine if it's excessive. You could free up hours every day, time you could spend on yourself, your career, your friends, or your family. On the other hand, you could make lasting enemies of every TV-addicted housemate. Make sure you notify (and maybe get a consensus from) your tube-watching loved ones before you ditch the set.

MORNING GLORY

THERE IS ONE TIME OF THE DAY when the phone never rings, the world keeps getting brighter, and you have the whole day ahead: early morning.

Did that sentence just set your teeth on edge? You very likely had an instinctive reaction to the phrase "early morning." You said to yourself, "I am not a morning person."

Some people certainly get up early more easily than others. But if you feel groggy first thing in the morning, that does not mean you are biologically incapable of getting up. In the days when most Americans farmed, *everybody* was a morning person. A dairy farmer would not roll over in bed at 4:00 A.M. and mutter to his wife, "I'm sorry, dear, but I can't milk the cows right now. I'm not a morning person." We all wage a continuing struggle against biology. Who is genetically suited to sitting at a desk all day or driving a cab for hours? A woman who's thinking of taking up jogging doesn't determine whether her oxygen uptake and slow-twitch musculature

Plus They Were Healthy, Wealthy, and Wise

He that riseth late, must trot all day, and shall scarce overtake his business at night. —POOR RICHARD

All memorable events . . . transpire in morning time and in a morning atmosphere. —HENRY DAVID THOREAU

I never thought that Adam had much advantage of us from having seen the world while it was new. . . . We see as fine risings of the sun as Adam ever saw. . . . —DANIEL WEBSTER

For fifty years he rose before the sun.
—PRESIDENT JOHN THORNTON KIRKLAND
of Harvard, speaking approvingly of
John Adams

make her a jogging person. Before spring cleaning we don't undergo psychological testing to see if we're cleanliness people. Yet we're perfectly willing to categorize ourselves as biologically unfit for dawn just because we're not one of those (extremely rare) people who bound out of bed, beam at their suffering mates, and shout, "Good morning! What are *your* plans for the day?"

Besides, if you need an alarm clock or a spouse to roust you out of bed, it probably isn't your genetic inheritance that makes you sleepy. Most adult Americans don't log enough Zs each night. If you are past the teenage years and under the age of sixty, you probably need seven or eight hours' sleep. If even seven doesn't seem enough—if you're drowsy after lunch or if getting out of bed feels like a death march—you should sleep an extra half hour to an hour at night. Most people who follow the same routine every weekday, going to bed at the same time and getting up at the same time, don't need alarms to get them up.

If you are getting enough sleep, you are more morning-adaptable than you think. You can fly from Los Angeles to Boston and cross three time zones, but you shudder at the thought of staying in one place and going to bed an hour early. Gaining a morning hour is a good deal easier, if you do it right, so easy that you might get ambitious and try for a little more. Here are four steps to becoming a certified morning person:

1. Mark Labor Day on your calendar as the beginning of your time-changing plan. On that day take stock of the amount of sleep you get at night. Before you begin rising earlier, make sure you're going to bed early enough on your old schedule. Spend a month getting used to a reasonable bedtime. Turn the television off an hour earlier, and read in bed for half an hour or so. Or close your eyes and listen to music. Establish a routine, a bedtime ritual. Unless television makes you sleepy, the routine probably should be tubeless; producers are masters at keeping you watching. Go to bed at the same time every weeknight. Don't stay up more than an hour late on most weekend nights. Avoid naps during this period, so you can feel sleepy when it's time to sleep. If at all possible, try to expose yourself to sun light in the morning. It helps reset your biological clock.

2. On the Friday before the end of daylight saving time, go to bed on a weekday schedule. Avoid alcohol and caffeine; they interfere with effective sleep. Consider turning dinner on Friday into a minor family celebration. Exchange gifts—bedtime books, sleeping caps, herbal tea—that signify coziness and home comforts.

Morning People's Mornings

Benjamin Franklin

Got up at five, washed, said a prayer, took a "tonic bath" by sitting naked while he read or wrote. Breakfast at eight. Business from eight to twelve.

Margaret Fuller

Starting at age fifteen, got up at five, walked for an hour, practiced piano, read philosophy and French. From nine-thirty to noon, studied Greek, practiced piano, "lounged" for half an hour.

Went on to cofound the transcendentalist magazine the *Dial,* married an Italian count, and died, tragically and romantically, in a shipwreck.

John Quincy Adams

Starting as a child and continuing until he died, got up at five and timed the sunrise.

Salmon P. Chase

As a noted abolitionist lawyer, rose at four-thirty. Prayers, Bible reading, work on speeches. Breakfast at seven. Began meeting clients at eight. Court at nine, meetings afterward.

Henry David Thoreau

Rose at sunrise (he wasn't big on clocks). Took a bath in Walden Pond. Cleaned the cabin. Went off on an adventure.

Girls in the mills of Lowell, Massachusetts, during the 1830s
Up at five, cold bath, off to work.

Louisa May Alcott

When she was eleven, her father, Bronson Alcott, founded a commune called Fruitlands near Harvard, Massachusetts. Louisa's typical morning: Up at five, cold bath. Singing lesson. Washed dishes. Went for a walk. Did spelling and math lessons. Listened to a story.

Babe Ruth

At the St. Mary's Industrial School for Boys got up at five. To chapel for mass. Then breakfast. Then school. Then shirtmaking shop. Then base-ball.

Daniel Webster

At his beloved Massachusetts farm, Marshfield, rose at three or four in the morning. Fed his cattle and then went to his library, worked until nine. Breakfast at ten. Afterward liked to say, "I have finished my day's work, written all my letters, and now I have nothing to do but enjoy myself."

In Washington rose at four, lit a fire, read or wrote until six, had breakfast, then walked to the city market for groceries.

Black abolitionist Charlotte Forten of Salem, Massachusetts, when she was sixteen

Up at five. Homework until breakfast. School. Wrote in journal.

Moral: The most productive habits are early ones.

3. On the following night, turn your clocks back an hour to standard time, the way you're supposed to. Now go to bed an hour early by the clock, and set your alarm an hour earlier than your usual weekday time. If your habitual bedtime is eleven, set your clocks back an hour and go to sleep when they say ten. Your body will feel as if it's eleven anyway.

If you set your weekday alarm for 6:30 A.M., reset it for 5:30 Sunday morning. It may seem strange getting up long before dawn, and you may spark comment from family members who smell coffee at such an hour, but to your body it should feel like a normal weekday morning. Do something you especially want to do, like driving an hour or two to your favorite state park, or watching a video, or cooking a leisurely breakfast for the family, or writing letters to friends.

That first morning may feel a little rugged, but if you plan it right, you will have gained several hours of weekend. If you're used to sleeping in—to, say, eight-thirty—you'll have three extra hours without any obligation, hours to spend entirely on yourself.

4. Keep your alarm set to that new time every weekday for a month. The hardest part will be avoiding the temptation to stay up at night. If you have an answering machine, set it to answer quickly before you go to bed. After a month of this routine you should be able to wake up at the new hour even if the alarm doesn't go off—provided you manage your bedtime routine well. Even if you stay up late on an occasional weekend night, your definition of "late" should have changed permanently. You may be—dare we say it?—a self-made morning person.

WINDFALL HOURS

SUPPOSE YOU HAVE actually learned to get up early. You can congratulate yourself on being a highly disciplined person. Now reward yourself with still more time as you head off for work. One way might be to take the bus.

You will not hear many people say that public transportation saves time. How could it? Door to door it probably is faster to hop in your car and drive than it is to wait for a bus or train. But going faster does not necessarily mean saving time. When you drive, you limit your options to spend traveling time on activities other than driving.

Imagine that it takes twenty minutes to drive to work, but an hour door to door by bus, when you count in the time you walk to the stop, wait for the bus to show up, transfer to another bus, and walk from the bus stop to work. Which is the more efficient use of your time?

The answer isn't as obvious as it seems. Suppose you don't get any exercise but would like to start small with a daily fitness routine. Twenty minutes on a treadmill at a health club could take an hour out of your day, once you've driven both ways and showered. A brisk walk to the bus might be enough of a substitute workout. So, while the bus takes you an extra eighty minutes a day in transportation time, it could save you sixty minutes of club time. The bus then puts you just twenty minutes behind a car drive in daily freedom.

Now suppose one of your additional goals is to read at least a dozen books a year. You find you don't have enough time at night to meet that goal. So you bring a book on the bus and spend twenty minutes reading each way, or forty minutes daily. The walking and reading now put you twenty daily minutes ahead of driving.

Obviously everyone has a different use for transportation time. Some people like listening to abrasive talk show hosts on the car radio. Others play book tapes, "reading" as they drive. Still others bring along tape recorders and dictate letters or their thoughts. Or they spend the time daydreaming. Mass transportation may be impractical or nonexistent where you live. In that case, driving may be your best option. But you can't be sure that

But They Lacked Frequent Flier Mileage

✦ Henry David Thoreau saved himself time and trouble by hardly ever leaving Concord, Massachusetts. His goal was to know thoroughly an area six miles square. "I have traveled a good deal in Concord," he asserted.

✦ Amherst resident Emily Dickinson was a fellow nontraveler. "To shut our eyes is Travel," she said. "The Seasons understand this."

Moral: What do you want from travel? Can you get it without going anywhere?

your own commuting time is useful until you do some accounting. If you drive to work, are you spending that time on meeting your goals? If not, deduct that time from your day; you're spending it just on driving. If there are alternative ways to get to work—including riding a bike, walking, or carpooling—does any of the resulting commuting time help you meet your goals? Subtract from this positive time the minutes that these alternative methods "waste"—time you have to spend showering or just plain traveling. Which form of transportation comes out ahead?

This approach can help you plan your longer trips better. Before you travel, estimate the amount of time you will have available to do what you want: reading, getting work done, watching an in-flight movie, taking a nap. If you find that traveling is a matter of waiting for the trip to end, try seeing it as personal time. If you take a long car trip alone, borrow some book tapes from your local library. Borrow or buy a cassette player if you don't have one in your car.

All these calculations assume you don't travel with spouse or children. A long trip with young kids cannot by any stretch of the imagination be considered personal time for you. In that case you have to consider the travel time as family time and plan accordingly. If you are used to family activities without television, then you probably know what to do already. Otherwise you will have to collaborate with family members and come up with a plan to keep children from killing each other. Or hope for an in-flight movie.

What are we doing when we see the potential of extra time in the parts of our lives—television, travel, our morning mental fog—that we once thought only *consumed* time? We have made a virtue of a weed. We have taken a hindrance, an obstacle, and made it work for us. In the next chapter you will see how the same notion can help us exploit one of the most useful obstacles of all, the bad habit.

CHAPTER 7

The Habitual Yankee

In which are revealed the virtues of the bad habit

B EING CREATURES OF HABIT makes us the planet's most adaptable species. Our bodies get used to things quickly. Cut way back on salt, and every restaurant meal and can of soup starts tasting salty. A Bostonian puts on a light sweater for the same temperature that drives a Miamian into gloves and scarf.

The body also plays the trick of habit with the sense of time. Stand next to a clock or watch that has a sweep second hand. Close your eyes, and count off twenty seconds as accurately as you can, saying, "one one thousand, two one thousand," and so on. Do this when you first get up, several hours later, after lunch, and at bedtime. If you are like most people, you counted too slowly first thing in the morning (if you could count then at all). You counted too fast at ten o'clock, slowed down at two, and then got more accurate before you went to bed. This little experiment can act as a kind of chronological mood ring, letting you see how keyed up you are at various times. (One drawback, of course, is that spouses and bosses tend to look askance at people who close their eyes and count when they're under pressure.) If every New Yorker performed this exercise on a regular basis, an entire city might begin walking more slowly, replacing the famous Manhattan stride with a leisurely stroll. "It is a great art to saunter," noted Henry David Thoreau.

What seems fast or slow depends on our perspective, a quality we can change.

Of course walking fast isn't necessarily a bad habit. A sin to one person is a virtue to another. But even those habits you consider bad have virtues of their own:

- ✦ If nothing else, habits reveal a lot about your inclinations.
- ✦ As we have seen, a time-consuming habit offers the promise of free time.
- ✦ Some bad habits aren't as bad as others and might properly be left alone—just as a good gardener doesn't try to remove every weed.

What makes a habit? Something you do regularly that you don't think about; something that would make you feel uneasy if you *didn't* do it. Good habits simplify. They boost you toward your goals, make your daily decisions for you, set parts of your life on autopilot. Bad habits complicate. The extreme versions, of course, are ruinous addictions. But even the less scary habits can sap time and push you backward, away from your goals.

Your body can get just as used to eating bran flakes as doughnuts every morning. It doesn't care whether you watch TV or read at bedtime. Either can be a habit that helps you go to sleep. In a bit we will talk more about bad habits and how to transform them into good ones. But you do not

Creatures of Habit

What maintains one vice would bring up two children. —POOR RICHARD

There is no more miserable human being than one in whom nothing is habitual but indecision. —WILLIAM JAMES

Eat plenty of roughage and use your brains. —LYDIA PINKHAM, whose profile still adorns the Lydia E. Pinkham Vegetable Compound, the most successful and long-lived patent medicine ever sold. Mrs. Pinkham attributed her family's unusually good health not to her medicine but to her daily advice.

need to seek and destroy every bad habit. That just complicates things. Instead concentrate more on the habits you *want*.

To see how much a creature of habit you really are, consider this exercise:

✦ Think of every single thing you do out of habit in the course of a day. Include good habits and bad, from brushing your teeth to biting your nails. Now rank the habits from best to worst.
✦ Think of every decision you have to make in a day: selection of morning radio station, clothing, food, restaurant, business decisions, television shows. Could you turn any of them into habits?
✦ Think of all your accomplishments yesterday. It doesn't have to be anything important—just something that got you toward a goal, or advanced you toward a deadline, or somehow made you feel you made progress. Could you do any of these things regularly?

HABITUAL SIMPLIFYING

H ERE ARE TWO HABIT-FORMING TECHNIQUES that might help unclutter your life and assist you in meeting goals. (More specific ones will appear in later chapters.)

Employ bad habits. Instead of trying to break all your unwanted habits, consider using some of them as cues to accomplish something else. Suppose you're a nail biter with gum trouble. The dentist warns you that root canal work is inevitable if you don't pay more attention to your gums. He tells you to improve your gums' circulation by "stimulating" them with orangewood toothpicks several times a day. Instead of writing little stick-um notes to yourself or tying a string on your finger, you "link" this new chore to your bad habit. Think of your nail biting as an

---

Or Was It Just the Nutmeg?

C ONNECTICUT NOW CALLS ITSELF the Constitution State and the Nutmeg State. But throughout the seventeenth and eighteenth centuries it was known as the Land of Steady Habits.

The state has registered more patents per capita than any other part of the world.

Moral: These two facts may have nothing to do with each other. Then again, maybe they do. The most creative, productive people in history stood on a solid floor of habit.

alarm clock: Every time you find a finger in your mouth, grab a toothpick and start stimulating.

Ratchet up. A ratchet is a device that allows progress and prevents backsliding. When you use your human instinct for habits, you take advantage of your tendency to get used to things. Someone who has lived in the city all his life often finds it difficult to fall asleep in the country. A person who keeps the car radio tuned to the classical station usually finds rap music jarring. If you eat only vegetarian, a Big Mac can seem truly disgusting.

You can ratchet up toward your goals. Suppose you haven't had a lick of exercise in years. Running three miles may seem daunting, to say the least. But start walking a mile three times a week for six months. Two-mile walks start seeming doable. Then three-mile walks. Maybe you start jogging some of the distance, then all of the distance, and a three-mile run doesn't seem crazy anymore. It seems . . . normal.

A person accustomed to getting up at 7:00 every morning will probably find a 5:00 A.M. wake-up call, well, alarming. But a few weeks of getting up at 6:30 makes 6:00 seem possible. And if 6:00 becomes the custom, then 5:30 isn't so terrible.

Ratcheting up is a means of making your goal seem normal. Establish the right long-term goal, figure on the habits it will take to get you there, and then give yourself time to build up to them.

There are various kinds of habits that you can put to work for your goals. The *personal habit* is the easiest to maintain, because it has to do with our bodies, and our bodies have a lot to do with our lives. Successful goals are like appendages. Good personal habits—brushing teeth, eating breakfast, bathing—maintain your appendages. Most people wouldn't think of avoiding brushing their teeth; such a habit succeeds because it has to do with our bodies. If you want to get in shape or manage your household finances, make exercise or balancing your checkbook seem similar to brushing your teeth. Set aside a regular place and time, and keep it up until you do it without thinking.

The *household habit* is a chore you have put on automatic pilot. Doing the dishes, making the bed, putting clothes away, anything you do automatically to fix things up around you is a household habit. One of the best ways to annoy a loved one is to acquire habits that conflict. She drapes her clothes over the bedroom chair at night; he hangs his in the closet, carefully guarding the crease in his pants. She can't bear seeing pots in the sink; he thinks it the height of efficiency to let them stack up and wash them all at once. Ask your spouse what annoys him the most, and consider changing your habits.

A third kind of habit has atrophied in America or maybe just changed beyond recognition. Let's call it the *habit of grace*. In an earlier time it was called manners. A few graceful habits hang on, quaintly; many of us still say "please" and "thank you" and even "bless you" automatically. If you don't think twice before letting a car pull ahead of yours from a side street, if you could not bear the thought of making someone wait for you for a restaurant date, if calling your loved one is the first thing to come to mind when you have to work late, then you are blessed with habits of grace.

GRACE AND COMMUNITY

THESE HABITS HAVE BECOME LESS VISIBLE because of great changes in every person's social web. Until the rise of the automobile a person's circle of acquaintances was determined largely by geography. Your community was where you lived. These days it is not quite so easy to determine your community. Our families are not all in one place. Our friends

Two Graceful Yankees

✦ In 1977 McCoy Stadium in Pawtucket, Rhode Island, was starting to fade. Home of the Triple A professional baseball Pawtucket Red Sox, the park was attracting one sixth its former total attendance. Rowdies had taken over the stands. Then Ben Mondor bought the stadium. He stood outside the entrance before the games and shook the hand of every person who walked in. (He and the team president Mike Tamburro also threw out more than a hundred toughs the first game of the season.) By 1991 attendance had set a record of 362,000.

✦ In 1862 Clara Barton set out for Antietam with a wagon train of supplies for wounded soldiers. The teamsters refused to take orders from a lady. On the first night the men refused to stop and finally pulled into camp at 9:00 P.M. Instead of throwing a fit, Barton made dinner for them and treated them with elaborate politeness. It worked: The teamsters were duly ashamed, apologized, and promised to try to get used to answering to a woman.

Moral: Grace is the best revenge.

may be scattered. Our professional contacts may be thousands of miles away. Our social network can be a mix of coworkers, relatives, neighbors, even professional colleagues who converse over the Internet.

Life might be simpler if we still lived near the people we felt closest to. Wouldn't it be great to be able to go "calling" on a Sunday afternoon, driving around and visiting our friends? What if we could find out about jobs, advance ourselves in our professions, and talk to local civic leaders and politicians all in one visit to a local tavern? Of course most of us don't have time to drive around on a Sunday afternoon, and maybe it's best if our politicians don't hang out in taverns. But we miss something of the community that our forebears felt. Our nation was built on that sense of togetherness; the American Revolution was planned in taverns after all.

Technology has greatly simplified the effort of staying in touch with people, and geography is no longer a barrier. Still, there is a difference between *communication* and *community*. Communications technology throws information at us; community is what gives us our sense of place in the world beyond our home. Few people would want to substitute the convenience of the telephone and fax machine with the quaintness of Sunday visits and the camaraderie of the tavern. But what if we could combine the best of twentieth-century technology and nineteenth-century community? Maybe what we miss is not the low-tech small-town life but the *habits of community* that once were a part of that life.

Let's look at the chief means that gentlefolk had of keeping in touch with one another within a community: the calling card, the note, and the letter.

YOUR NAME ON A SILVER PLATTER

W HEN UPPER-CRUST NEW ENGLANDERS stopped frequenting taverns, they needed a way to keep their social connections strong. So began the practice of "calling." Most commonly reserved for Sunday after church, calling meant going to friends' houses and paying them short visits. If your friends were out calling as well, you left a calling card: your name, printed on heavy stock and left with a servant or beside the door. People had small silver plates to hold cards, as a kind of index of one's standing in society. The more visits, the more prestigious the visitors, the higher the social rank of the person being called on.

Most people these days would consider the practice an annoyance. Who has time to receive drop-in visitors, let alone go visiting?

On the other hand, the practice of calling has not disappeared. The telephone has replaced the horse and buggy, and the answering machine serves as a high-tech calling card platter. Through these devices people still "visit" with one another and leave evidence of themselves if no one is home. What if you made a list of, say, a dozen or so friends and relatives and reserved half an hour one evening a week for social calling? Assuming you were willing to pay the long-distance bills, you could call three or four of the people on your list. The following week you could call the next three or four, and so on. If you get their answering machines, you could leave messages saying, "I just thought I'd say hello. Nothing

---

And He Would Have
Loved Voice Mail

ARK TWAIN was not enamored of the telephone, but in 1878 he had one of the world's first private home phones installed in his Hartford, Connecticut, mansion. When the line went in, he said, "The voice carries entirely too far as it is. If Bell had invented a muffler or a gag, he would have done a real service."

Moral: Some transcendent souls don't need technology. Twain's voice carried all the way into the next century.

important. Don't feel you have to return my call." That way you could ensure yourself of getting in touch with each of the dozen at least once a month.

A WONDER OF TECHNOLOGY:
THE SHORT NOTE

THERE ARE OTHER MEANS of maintaining remote-control relationships, and they, too, involve a combination of postmodern technology and Victorian manners. When Margaret Fuller stayed as a guest at the home of Ralph Waldo Emerson, the two great transcendentalists kept to their separate floors during most of the day but wrote each other notes carried by servants. In those times it would have been scandalous for a man to be alone with a woman in a room; Emerson and Fuller saw each other mostly at mealtimes, when other people were present. The notes also allowed them to "visit" with each other while leaving time and privacy for their work. Miss Fuller and Mr. Emerson were not unusual. People sent messages to each other across town; a pair of friends would exchange four or five notes in a day.

If that seems strange to us, what would these two Victorians have thought about fax machines? Or electronic mail? They might have known exactly what to do once they got the hang of the technology. While offices often frown on socializing by fax, the machine is suited for just the sort of note exchanging that Emerson and Fuller did. You write a message, stick it into the contraption, dial a number, and the note is received almost instantly. The recipient can respond at her leisure.

Electronic mail works pretty much the same way, provided that all parties have a computer with access to the Internet. The Net allows people to send notes to individuals or to whole groups of people. Most professions

How George Bush Became Notable

A S A BOY GROWING UP IN CONNECTICUT, George Herbert Walker Bush learned to write notes on every possible occasion. When he got older, the volume of letters increased, and his writing became a kind of reflex action. He banged away at his manual typewriter every time a friend or a relative (or even a distant acquaintance) got sick or had a birthday or an anniversary. When someone wrote him, he wrote right back, no matter who it was.

Bush gained an unusually large circle of friends that way, a useful resource in his business and politics. He developed a wide reputation for thoughtfulness. After he was elected president of the United States, the note writing continued, and it earned him an even better reputation: as a politician who was actually human.

Moral: George Bush was still writing notes long after letters went out of fashion. He carried out one of the great principles of simple living: He exceeded low expectations.

conduct ongoing discussions via computer, and with a little searching you can find endless conversation on nearly every avocation known to humans. Although computers are far from cheap, access to the Internet costs less than most people's minimum-service phone bill. As more people gain access to the Internet, we are likely to see the rise of "virtual taverns," electronic gathering places where people can share news, advice, and gossip—and engage in habits of community.

AND THEN THERE ARE PERSONS OF LETTERS

A LL THIS TECHNOLOGY does not adequately substitute for the charm of the handwritten personal letter, which remains the most user-friendly, if slowest, form of modern communication. Letter writing is not a lost art. People still practice it; they just do it far less often than before. There is value in scarcity; the fewer the letters written and sent, the more their recipients appreciate them. Nothing is more courteous and respectful than a note. It requires time and thought to write, but little effort to read. And unlike a fax or phone call, it does not interrupt.

Habits of grace and community can be especially useful, as we shall see in the next chapter, in which we acquire helpmeets in our goals and allies to our calling.

CHAPTER 8

Helpmeets

In which the reader learns the art of superior attachment

TOO OFTEN THE PEOPLE AROUND US make our lives seem more messy than simple. They steal our time, burden us with guilt, boss us around. The only way to rid ourselves of human complications is to become a hermit. But being a hermit rarely brings a good salary.

Instead of daydreaming about an escape from people, we can seek helpmeets in finding our callings and meeting our goals. These useful people come in three varieties: heroes, mentors, and lovers. While lovers tend to get most of our attention, we are more likely to find our calling in heroes, especially those who seem like real, ordinary people, such as Rosa Parks or Paul Revere. "The hero is commonly the simplest and obscurest of men," Thoreau said. That makes it possible to apply their heroism to our own obscure lives.

Unlikely Heroines

✦ Prudence Crandall of Canterbury, Connecticut, allowed a black girl to enroll in her female boarding school during the 1830s. The town uproar over this unprecedented integration forced the school to close. So Miss Crandall created an academy for blacks only. In 1833 the state reacted by passing the Black Law, which forbade schools to educate out-of-state colored people. Miss Crandall was arrested and jailed. Mobs wrecked the building. She married and moved to Kansas, where she continued teaching African Americans. In 1886, lobbied by Mark Twain, an apologetic Connecticut legislature voted her a pension of four hundred dollars a year.

✦ The *Atlantic Monthly* reviewed Emily Dickinson's poetry in 1892: "An eccentric, dreamy, half-educated recluse in an out-of-the-way New England village—or anywhere else—cannot with impunity set at defiance the laws of gravitation and grammar. . . . Oblivion lingers in the immediate neighborhood."

✦ Emma Willard moved with her husband to Middlebury, Vermont, where he was headmaster of an academy. A nephew went with them to study at Middlebury College. Women were forbidden to study at Middlebury, so Mrs. Willard read all of her nephew's textbooks. She got enough of an education to start a school for girls in 1814, which eventually moved to Troy, New York. To this day the Emma Willard School pioneers in teaching academics, as well as independence, to girls.

Moral: Heroes often remain obscure during much of their lifetime because their heroism transcends their time.

The people who become your heroes help determine your own brand of heroism. When you follow their example, you are approaching your own calling. During the exercises in Chapter 3, did pictures of other people come to mind? Can you imagine yourself as a hero, boldly going where no one has gone before? Thinking in this way may allow you to attach some meaning to your habits. You might visualize yourself as the subject of a documentary or newsreel. ("He did twenty sit-ups *every morning* because his wife likes firm abs!" "She wrote all her thank-you letters *the day after Christmas!*")

A Dartmouth professor once agreed to teach a course in Greek to a single student. "Why are you wasting your time on just one kid?" a colleague asked the prof. "To save his immortal soul!" he shouted in reply. It is not a sin to think of your habits transcendently. The idea is a little dramatic, maybe, but it also gets pretty quickly to several central tenets of heroism and simplicity: Do your habits lead to what's important to you? Can you visualize the wondrous results if you continue with—or change—them? Are you saving your immortal soul?

The vision doesn't have to seem dramatic to other people. There is a small dose of heroism in the cleaning lady who sends three children to college, or in the man who fights to convert a town road easement into a hiking trail, or in the woman who gives up her worldly goods and enters a convent. By carrying out their callings with bravery and purpose, they may inspire just one other person, or maybe only themselves. They may be teachers with one student.

Then there are the helpmeets called mentors. You learn not so much from their accomplishments as from their knowledge. While a hero acts, a mentor *knows*.

You don't have to work very hard to get a mentor. You need only choose one.

CHOOSING A MENTOR

D O YOU WANT to get ahead in your profession? Then a boss, a colleague, or a member of the profession might provide ready-made mentoring.

Are you searching for some meaning in your life? Look around you for a spiritual mentor. Whole professions are devoted to this—the ministry and rabbinate, for instance.

You may want to become a better parent or lover. Good parents and lovers are everywhere (although their children and lovers may hesitate to admit it).

Or you may use a mentor to learn a new skill or become a better artist or musician or to become a better athlete or just get fitter. If you're of a certain age, it helps to acquire a mentor who is a bit older and has suffered the pains and injuries you're in danger of.

How can you pay for the advice and help? Sometimes the pleasure and plain ego gratification of mentoring someone are enough. On the other hand, an occasional invitation to dinner isn't a bad idea. You can also barter a skill of your own, from programming a VCR to clipping hedges.

A mentor may be below you in your office hierarchy or junior to you in age. If your first computer just landed on your desk, for example, a secretary may be the best person to teach you how to use it. Mentors show up among friends, relatives, teachers—anyone who does what you want to do. Early in their lives most people see a parent or two as mentors. This is fine, but an offspring needs mentor supplements. Too often parents look to their children as improved versions of themselves. They may fail to recognize when their kids actually succeed.

Spouses or lovers make equally good, if risky, mentors. It helps if each partner has something to teach the other. But close relationships can get touchy when the protégé has learned all that the mentor has to teach.

Mentors and Their Protégés

Susannah Wheatley and Phillis Wheatley

Slavers kidnapped Phillis Wheatley at the age of seven from her home in Senegal and brought her to Boston, where a tailor, John Wheatley, bought her. His wife, Susannah, took a shine to the girl and had her educated. Within two years Phillis was reading English and Latin literature and writing poetry. In 1773 Susannah sent her to England, where she became a darling of London society and published a highly acclaimed collection of *Poems on Various Subjects, Religious and Moral.*

Ben Franklin and Cotton Mather

When Franklin was a teenage Boston apprentice, he liked to visit Mather, who was ready with advice (and a few coins) for bright young men. One day Mather was seeing Franklin out when they passed under a low beam. "Stoop, stoop!" Mather said, but Franklin smacked his head against the beam. The old Puritan couldn't resist a homily. "You are young, and have the world before you," Mather said. "Stoop as you go through it, and you will miss many hard bumps."

Ben Franklin and the Gout

As an old man Franklin had no equals, let alone mentors. He found superior wisdom in his gout. He wrote a dialogue between himself and the ailment that admonished the man for complaining of the pain. "Is it not I who, in the character of your physician, have saved you from the palsy, dropsy, and apoplexy?" says the Gout. "One or the other of which would have done for you long ago but for me."

Athena and Telemachus

As every educated New Englander once knew, the first mentor was Mentor, an old man who advised Telemachus, son of Odysseus, in Homer's *Odyssey*. Mentor was really Athena, goddess of wisdom. Interesting how the first mentor was a woman. Here she was a goddess, and she had to dress as a man to get that boy to pay attention.

Moral: A great mentor sometimes looks different from you and comes without warning.

YOUR MENTOR: AN OWNER'S MANUAL

USE YOUR NEWLY ACQUIRED MENTOR for what you most want to improve in your life, including *technique*. Presumably your mentor is better than you are at what you want to do. Look for situations in which you find yourself blocked, unable to move ahead with your goal. Maybe you're having problems confronting a coworker, finding time to exercise, dealing with temptation. How does your mentor handle these situations?

Watch not just the mentor's technique but also her *attitude,* the expression on her face as she deals with moments that would be tough for you. Can you see yourself in her situation? A mentor can teach you without even knowing it. As Casey Stengel said, you can observe a lot just by looking.

Besides technique and attitude, you need to know how your mentor *manages time* and *disciplines* herself. You may need to ask some questions to get this information. How long did it take her to reach the point you aspire to? What did she give up along the way? How much time did she spend on achieving her (and your) goal? Per day? Per week? Per month?

Your mentor helps you most of all with *inspiration*. He shows you that it is possible to do what you want to do. It's been done! You don't feel alone with your goal. For every setback, every failure, every discouraging word, you can see a living refutation. You're not crazy after all (or, if you are, you have excellent company).

A good mentor is not always encouraging, however. You don't need just praise; you need feedback, someone to tell you in a positive way when you're screwing up. A mentor can be a yardstick or benchmark. You measure yourself against that person's example. Competitive people know this instinctively: If you want to improve your game, play a superior opponent.

With the right exemplars, you may do more than pursue your goals. You may even simplify your life. Who can help you set priorities better than the people you admire? They help anchor you, almost as much as a good family does. That brings us to . . .

THE EFFICIENT LOVER

"THE IDEAL HUSBAND," wrote an elderly woman to *Yankee*® magazine some years ago, "is a man who is careful of his clothes; don't drink no spirits; can read the Old Testament without spelling out the words; and can eat a cold dinner on wash day to save the women folks from cooking."

As this wise woman knew, everything, even love, can be simplified—with the proper self-discipline. It is all well and good to get carried away, vow eternal loyalty and affection, and abuse the patience of friends and coworkers with testimony on the inamorata's charms. Such zeal is natural; some scientists think it may be hormonally dictated. But if you're looking for a lifetime relationship, you need to be more hardheaded about romantic acquisitions. Consider following this principle: **Acquiring a lover is like buying a camp in Maine.**

There are differences, of course. Camps require more taxes but less maintenance: You just take the dock out of the water, drain the pipes if the cabin has plumbing, and lock up for the season. Still, camps and lovers spark similar irrational emotions, and a simple strategy is essential to keep you from regretting your decisions. In Chapter 4 we discussed the principles of buying a camp in Maine:

+ The bigger the target, the easier it is to hit.
+ A miss is information, not failure.

And remember the "satisfaction" moral:

+ When counting your blessings, round up.

A woman could probably find a reasonable number of men who can read the Old Testament without getting stuck. The available population of nondrinking Old Testament readers is considerably smaller, but still a hittable target. Note that the elderly woman in *Yankee®* magazine did not set us up for disappointment by mentioning looks, bank account, or access to the information superhighway. With the wisdom of her years she limited the criteria and kept the target big.

The second camp-buying criterion, the part about the informative miss, is what single men and women employ when they go on dates. The Puritans weren't big on dating. They didn't have to go out to dinner to learn what they needed to know about a potential spouse. If we were looking only for Bible-toting teetotalers, we probably wouldn't have that much need for dates ourselves. But if we have set somewhat narrower targets, evenings out with the opposite sex produce two forms of information: whether the candidates hit your target and whether your target is reasonably attainable.

MARRIED BLITZ

IMMEDIATELY AFTER THE CIVIL WAR a group of women known as the Mercer Girls went to great lengths—seven thousand miles, actually—to hit their marital target. They were a strange cargo—five hundred young women from all over New England—that set sail from the East Coast in 1865 for Seattle, Washington. The genius behind the voyage was a merchant named Asa Mercer. Placing what must have been the world's most effective personals ad, Mercer got lonely bachelors to pony up three hundred dollars, enough for the voyage and a tidy profit. The first couple got hitched within a week of the women's arrival. Ecstatic residents elected Mercer to the Washington Assembly, but not before he had married one of the women himself.

If this story appalls you, consider that each lonely bachelor and hopeful lady undoubtedly started out with one of the prime ingredients of a successful marriage: low expectations. The main criterion was that the partner be unmarried and of the opposite sex, qualities in short supply on both sides of the continent. With expectations like that, a new spouse had every opportunity to be pleasantly surprised.

The most successfully married Mercer Girls and Boys also followed the advice of Poor Richard:

She Also Saved the Cost of a Personals Ad

THE TOMBSTONE for the late Jared Bates, erected in 1800, reads: "His Widow Aged 24 who mourns as one who can be comforted lives at 7 Elm Street this village and possesses every qualification for a Good Wife."

Moral: To a good Yankee, nearly every stroke of fate is an improvable opportunity.

They Did It to Their Credit

———➤●◄———

S HERMANS HILL, RHODE ISLAND, once had the local name of Shift Hill. Widows used the site to remarry while wearing nothing but their shifts. The weddings took place at night, and they symbolized the brides' "nakedness" in marriage, freeing their second husbands of the debts of the first.

Moral: While the symbolism would not go over big these days, the concept of shedding past encumbrances is a pretty good simplifying principle.

"Keep your eyes wide open before marriage; half shut afterwards." The time to be rational is before you make a major life decision. Once you have made it, you can be as sentimental as you want.

Most people, of course, take the opposite approach. Before marriage they see nothing but perfection in a future mate; after, the flaws become painfully visible. This is a foolish approach to life, but nearly everyone takes it. Scientists are probably right to blame it on biology.

This isn't to say that any marriage can't stand some improvement. A little positive change can eliminate some of the white noise in your life. But improving a marriage is not easy. It is hard enough for a person to achieve goals by herself; getting another committed to the same goals, and to acquiring the right habits to meet them, is something else again. It is like the old marriage counselor's version of the lightbulb joke:

How many marriage counselors does it take to change a lightbulb?

That depends. Does the bulb want to be changed? (A counselor would also ask, "Where's the other bulb?")

The bulb may not want fixing because it ain't broke. From your

---

She Suffered in His Silence

C ALVIN COOLIDGE WROTE ABOUT HIS WIFE, Grace, in his autobiography: "For almost a quarter of a century she has borne with my infirmities and I have rejoiced in her graces."

Moral: If every spouse remained aware of his infirmities and rejoiced in his spouse's graces, there would be many more satisfied couples.

---

spouse's point of view, everything may be fine already. If that's not *your* point of view, you have some convincing to do. Or maybe your expectations are too high. Is your partner's figure less than Greek? Is his chin a little weak? Then, short of plastic surgery, maybe your spouse needs to change less than you or your attitude. It is extremely difficult to improve a spouse, who may in any case resent suggestions in that direction.

On the other hand, a marriage can be improved if both bulbs—sorry, spouses—want the change. Consider the procedures set out in Chapter 4 for setting goals. What exactly do you want out of a marriage? How much can you reasonably expect? What would satisfy you? How can you communicate these wishes without an explosion?

The chief answer is to go through the process together. But before you can do that, you should be sure that you both have an important skill for maintaining a good marriage: *Know how to argue.* It is a primary marital aid.

"Are you *kidding?*" asks the nervous reader. "I *hate* to argue. I spend half my time giving in just to avoid argument."

In New England right up through most of the nineteenth century you weren't considered fully educated unless you knew how to argue. Citizens devoted years of schooling to the subject, called rhetoric; it was foremost among the liberal arts. This is hard to believe today; we have an unfortunate aversion both to rhetoric and to the very notion of argument. Maybe we should reconsider this attitude if only for the reason that marriages don't last as long as they used to. (Rhetoric is not the only skill that sustains a marriage, of course, but bear with us for the sake of argument.) The Greeks invented rhetoric, and New Englanders adored the Greeks. Most of all they loved Aristotle, who wrote the book on argument.

ARISTOTLE'S PRINCIPLES
FOR GOOD MARITAL ARGUMENT

A CTUALLY HE WROTE A BOOK called *Rhetoric,* and his advice was directed toward the democratic management of a city-state. But his theories work at least as well with marital relations, and educated Yankee couples followed those notions to their benefit. After all, managing a marriage is no less difficult than managing a nation. So let us look at the *Rhetoric* as a marriage manual. To do so, you need learn only three Greek words. After employing them in marital argument, you can use them to impress your friends (and they come in handy in the workplace, as we shall see in Chapter 11).

Aristotle listed three basic elements to an effective argument. Being Greek, he listed them in his native language:

Ethos. This is the arguer's reputation. If your spouse trusts and respects you, he is much more open to persuasion. If you're lacking in ethos, that may be the main problem with your marriage. Why doesn't your spouse respect you? Is it because you have violated a trust in the past? Then you have to earn it back, a lengthy process. Is it because you always give in and never argue? Then it is time to begin arguing, standing up for what is important and ignoring the details (we'll get to that). Aristotle put ethos first because you can't get a good argument started without the listener's respect.

Pathos. This is your knowledge of the needs and emotions of your "audience," in this case your partner. What are the other person's needs? What does she want to hear? What is she likely to say in response? What will get her angry, or romantic, or frustrated, or make her laugh? *Pathos* is a root word for "sympathy." Recently whole books have been devoted to the difference in the ways that males and females communicate. Men tend to think in terms of winning and losing arguments. Women, on the other hand, consider a conversation successful if it brings two people closer. Men want to get to the point, to explain their overwhelming logic and then call it quits. Women often talk in a more roundabout way, gaining relationships rather than points. You give good pathos when you take into account your partner's way of arguing. The man should understand that the end point of most marital arguments is not winning the argument but improving the relationship, even when he's clearly right. The woman should look for the logic within the conversation and keep in mind where it's heading; that way she has a stake in solving problems.

Logos. This means the actual words of the argument in which logic comes in. Aristotle said the purpose of every logical argument should be not to win the battle but to discover what is best for all parties. He was not a great believer in compromise—that is, people giving in and coming up with some mutually unsatisfactory deal. Instead he argued for a consensus, which he defined as the "greater good." In a consensus everyone is supposed to win in the long run. A consensual marital argument aims its logic toward the good of the marriage, not toward the benefit of one or the other spouse. That should be the chief topic of every important argument between partners: What is good for the marriage? You compromise when you settle an argument over Saturday activities by devoting half the activities to shopping and half to a walk in the park. You reach a consensus if you agree to skip shopping and walking to dig up the garden. Compromise is give-and-take. It tends to focus on relatively petty details, on territory and who gets what. A consensus seeks benefit for everyone without regard to who benefits most. It focuses on what's important over the long run.

People took Aristotle's advice for more than two thousand years (even though there is no record of his having had a particularly successful marriage himself). As every educated Yankee once knew, two-thousand-year-old advice is worth listening to. Cultured New Englanders knew the difference between arguing and bickering. While bickering is pointless, a good argument comes to a point, a good relationship.

WHERE TO HAVE AN ARGUMENT

THE SIMPLEST OF MARRIAGES rests on a mutual sense of where the partners want to take the relationship and what they are willing to do to get there—goals and targets, in other words. But that is logos, and first you have to deal with ethos and pathos. Before you attack the argument itself, consider retreating. If you have kids, try to ditch them with a friend or relative. It might help to go someplace for a day and a night—an inn or a bed-and-breakfast, say—where you can go on walks and have some private conversation. If you stay at home, spend some time the day before fixing up a retreat area. Build a fire if you have a fireplace. Move the furniture around to make an enclosed nook. Change your surroundings to gain a fresh venue. It's best if both of you get involved somehow in the preparation.

Ethos is your first order of business, establishing the ways you like and respect each other. Don't dwell on the problems at this point. Count your blessings, and round up. List on a piece of paper what you like most about your partner physically, spiritually, mentally. Now list what you think are your own best assets that you offer your spouse. When each of you has two lists prepared, swap them (don't show anything until you're both done). How close are the lists? Any points of disagreement? Can you rank your spouse's attributes in order of importance to you? This is a great way at getting to the pathos: You tell your partner a lot when you rank what most turns you on.

How close does the list come to a description of the ideal Boy or Girl Scout? A Scout is supposed to be trustworthy, loyal, helpful, friendly, courteous, kind, obedient, cheerful, thrifty, brave, clean, and reverent. Add "good lover," and you have the ideal spouse as well, don't you?

For the logos, think about your goals for this year and over the next five years. Ask these questions:

Do you want to keep living where you are?
Do you expect the addition of any children?
Should either of you try to change jobs?
Over the next five years what do you most want to accomplish together?

It's often hard to talk about these things, so don't expect to launch flawlessly into a rational discussion. Think of the times you have had good, serious conversations, and try to duplicate the circumstances. Was it over dinner in a restaurant? A walk? A moment of delicious boredom? It also wouldn't hurt to decide on your agenda in advance. For your first retreat, consider just one item of discussion—say, how each of you wants to live five years from now and what it would take to get there. Build in plenty of time for silence, exercise, goofing around, or romance. Again, both of you should know what is on the agenda. If one of you secretly plans on romance and the other on a brisk hike, you could end up in an argument that has little to do with Aristotle.

MARITAL PRINCIPLES

WHETHER IN A RETREAT OR JUST TALKING with your spouse at any time, keep in mind the following principles for sustaining a marriage. **Know how to argue** is the first one.

Secondly, **always tell your spouse what you want.** Never blame your partner for failing to be a mind reader. Do you want flowers? Say you want flowers. Do you want cowboy boots for your birthday? Let it be known. Otherwise chances are good that you won't get what you want, and your loved one will have failed a test he didn't even know he was taking. Do you want to quit your job? Consult your partner first. Have you accomplished something you're proud of, or do you want your partner to notice your new clothing? Don't ever say, "Notice anything different?" Point it out. Silence is not always golden.

Thirdly, **count your blessings out loud.** If you see the slightest improvement in a partner, praise it. That positive reinforcement business actually works in some cases. If a husband gets rid of a small portion of spare tire, tell him how fit he is looking. If a wife changes a tire, praise her mechanical skill. Bring these improvements up when you hold your retreat. Discuss what brought about the change. Go into detail with your praise. Admire something specific about the improvement: the impressive outline of the pectorals or the fine detailing in a piece of sewing.

In Chapter 10 we discuss financial retreats, to help take the agony out of talking about money. Is there a big decision you need to make together: a possible move, or job change, or choice of school for a child? The point of a retreat is to take the pressure off decisions, to make your choices when the phone isn't ringing and no small person is hanging off your leg.

After you have been on a retreat, you need to do some maintenance, to check up on new habits and to see if targets are being met or have to be set back. If you've set a loose five-year plan, consider taking a few hours each year to update it. This could entail a retreat once a year. An alternative is to set a date—New Year's Eve, your anniversary, some obscure holiday—and go for a walk or huddle in some private space. Do the goals still seem realistic? Are your priorities in order?

DENYING THE SENSES

THIS THOUGHT MAY OCCUR TO YOU: What if you go on your retreat and discover you have nothing to say? What if you don't have any plans and don't care to acquire any? Worst of all, what if everything is going fine? Don't worry. You need only switch to another meeting technique: interspousal communication enhanced by sensory deprivation, aka pillow talk. When couples get together for a good time they often, out of sheer habit, look for stimulation—a movie, a restaurant dinner, bowling, that sort of thing. This works fine when you're seventeen; it is hard at that age to do anything with the opposite sex that *doesn't* stimulate you. Later in life, though, some couples find that the time they get along best is when they lie in the dark at bedtime and just talk. The reason many couples don't do this is that every minute of conversation is time spent not sleeping, and most of us get too little sleep as it is. Besides, there are few things more annoying than to have a partner drop off just when you're phrasing some profound thought.

Maybe we need something that gives us the advantages of pillow talk without the problem of exhaustion.

If both partners work, it might be a treat just to stay home. If you have kids, can you swap for a few hours with another family or pay the sitter to host them? An alternative would be to restrict the children to one floor—with a sitter, if possible—while keeping yourself to another. The ideal arrangement would be a soundproof underground bunker with a fireplace, but too few people have one.

Somehow ensconce yourselves in some quiet place. Once you get over the novelty of having quiet and privacy, you may find that you have absolutely nothing to say. This is perfectly understandable. If you're not in the habit of talking to each other, why would a quiet room make you start? There are several solutions:

1. Bask in the boredom. Limit the time to half an hour. Decide in advance that you won't mind the lack of stimulation. Sit next to each other, saying nothing if nothing comes to mind. Call it meditation.

> # Mather Glimpses Paradise
>
> ⸻✦⸻
>
> THE SUNDAY AFTER Cotton Mather married Katharine Philips in 1686, he preached a Boston sermon on "Divine Delights." Katharine bore him nine of his fifteen children.
>
> **Moral:** Mather could find rapture on earth. Of course, it is not recorded what Katharine thought of the experience.

2. Get a good bottle of wine and a candle. Stare soulfully into each other's eyes. Laugh. Stare soulfully at the bottle.

3. Try reading to each other. Collections of letters are good because you can read them in small chunks. Does the whole thing embarrass you? Who cares? No one is watching! Nineteenth-century couples did this for hours,

and look how low their divorce rate was. (Okay, reading aloud probably had nothing to do with the divorce rate, but it's still an admirable activity.)

All this supports a fourth marital principle that can apply to other aspects of your life: **Boredom is a good antidote to stress.** Few things are more salutary for complicated living than the times when you deprive your senses of stimulation. Is your spouse particularly unstimulating? Perfect! In fact, boredom is one of several excellent marital habits.

GOOD MARITAL HABITS

Savor moments of sweet boredom. We've already described the benefits (and don't wish to bore you; that's up to your partner).

Give gifts habitually. Call this habit permanent wooing. On regular occasions—from once a week to once a month—bring your partner something she particularly likes. Flowers are perfect, not just for women but for many men as well. Link the gift getting with another regular duty, such as filling your car's tank with gas. When you get gas, get flowers. The gifts don't have to cost much; even one flower will do. The point is simply to refresh the connection between you, to establish a small dutiful habit of grace.

Set bedtime ten minutes earlier than usual. Turn the television off. Spend the time talking—or not talking, as the case may be.

Listen for the sake of listening. When you come across a disagreement with your partner or a problem you both need to work out, schedule a special time for good argument. If you're the female partner, making an appointment gives the man the opportunity to feel he's not wasting time. If you're the man, try this revolutionary conversational technique: *Shut up.* Men talk a great deal more than women do, but they think they talk a good deal less. (Men compensate for this annoying trait by ensuring that everything they say is logical and to the point, but too few women have the perspicacity to notice.)

All this assumes that you can carve out the time to pay attention to your mate. If you have children, this mutual attention is even more important. But then your time is even scarcer. You're in serious need of management advice, which the next chapter offers.

CHAPTER 9

Offspring

On those factors of chaos called children

ARRIET BEECHER STOWE might have glittered even more as a literary star had she remained single. At a low moment she wrote her sister: "Since I began this note, I have been called off at least a dozen times; once for the fish man to buy a codfish; once to see a man who had brought me some barrels of apples; once to see a book man; then, to Mrs. Upham to see about a drawing I promised to make for her; then to nurse the baby; then into the kitchen to make a chowder for dinner; and now I am at it again, for nothing but deadly determination enables me ever to write. It is rowing against wind and tide."

Nothing complicates life so much as children, and Mrs. Stowe had six of them with her in that kitchen. Few of us are quite so fecund, but our parenting duties are no easier. Our own mistaken attitudes are partly to blame.

Modern society tends to hold parents solely responsible for their offspring's happiness and long-term stability. This is a very far cry from Puritans, who taught that infants arrived at birth already contaminated by sin. "In Adam's fall/We sinned all" are the first lines in *The New England Primer.* Back in those days no one thought to blame adults for juvenile delinquency.

In contrast, a modern primer slogan might read, "When your kid gets caught, it's all your fault." We wouldn't want to practice the Puritans' harsh discipline, but that original sin notion had its good points. If your kid is rotten, he's your begotten, but he also comes with the stuff of an original personality that takes you at least partly off the hook. So stop thinking blame and guilt. Instead improve your parenting opportunity. You need little more than the best of intentions and some simple principles.

A Part Hepburn Turned Down

BEING A HOUSEWIFE and a mother is the biggest job in the world, but if it doesn't interest you, don't do it. It didn't interest me, so I didn't do it.

—KATHARINE HEPBURN
in *People* magazine

THE FIRST PARENTAL PRINCIPLE:
If You Think You Know What You're Doing, Then You Probably Don't

THERE IS ONE PERFECT WAY to raise each individual child, but it is impossible to know what it is.

There is a vast body of research on childhood development, and it is

Moral Authorities

✦ The Puritans had few sentimental attitudes toward their offspring. Even as late as the mid-eighteenth century John Adams was adjuring his wife, Abigail, to rid the evil in their little children's minds. "Root out every little Thing," he wrote her. "Weed out every Meanness." One way to do that, he thought, was to "raise their Wishes—Fix their Attention upon great and glorious Objects."

✦ Other Bostonians of the time took the opposite tack. One of the most popular books in the famous old Boston Athenaeum library is an autobiography by the notorious eighteenth-century criminal James Allen. The book is bound in Allen's own skin—at the request of one of Allen's victims, whose descendant donated the book to the Athenaeum. The volume was used for years to spank naughty children, "on the theory," according to Cleveland industrialist Nathaniel D. Chapin, "that the skin of a bad man was particularly adapted to warming [the backside of] a small child."

Moral: What weeds out "Meanness" in one child may have just the opposite effect in another.

good for new parents to read some of the literature, if only to assure themselves that the bizarre and demanding creature they have brought into the world is indeed a member of the same species. But the problem with child psychology is that it fails to conform with a basic tenet of modern science: that an experiment is valid only if the results can be replicated. You can learn a great deal from the careful study of a single child. But then the next kid comes along and you might as well throw the data out the window. Does one child blossom under a supportive but restraint-free environment? The same treatment turns another into a spoiled monster. Does one thrive in competitive sports, excel when the parent stands shouting on the sidelines? The other melts in embarrassment and shame. Would one benefit from being ordered to eat everything on her plate? The same rule could turn the other anorexic. And it's *all your fault.*

If every child were alike, this chapter could consist of a single set of rules, and you would be guaranteed happy and productive offspring to support you in your dotage. But because kids don't have the decency to conform, we will introduce:

THE SECOND PARENTAL PRINCIPLE:
Principles Are Better Than Rules

A RULE IS MORE SPECIFIC THAN A PRINCIPLE; it tells exactly what to do. "Don't exceed fifty-five miles per hour on an urban highway." That's a rule. A principle, on the other hand, requires thought, not obedience. **Drive safely.** That's a principle. Principles are more flexible than rules. They allow latitude for us to select appropriate behavior and thus become principled.

Principles are essential to child rearing. You need something to fall back on when your kid suddenly collapses, writhing, onto a shopping mall floor in an attempt to extort a toy. A rule on this occasion might be: "Smile blithely, say brightly, 'That's not *my* child,' and pretend to walk off." After a few minutes' suspense the kid may very well get up and follow you, having learned never to repeat the offense. This rule has actually been known to work. The problem is what to do if the kid calls your bluff, screams even more loudly, and attracts the attention of mall security. To cover all contingencies requires a principle, not a rule. In this case a good principle might be: **Antisocial behavior doesn't belong in society.** Pick a screaming kid up, and make him sit in a quiet corner, as far from people as possible. Note how this principle can apply to an obnoxious child at home, at someone else's house, or on the playground.

A rule-based life is overly complicated. It takes an infinite number of rules to cover every situation. You can say, "When you take a test in school, don't look at your neighbor's answers." That's a rule, and a pretty sound one. But what if the kid accidentally discovers the answers in her own desk? Wouldn't she be better off with an overarching principle, such as **You're not a cheater?** A kid who believes in that principle can make up her own rules as she goes. Principles are easier to explain; rules are often harder to justify. If you find yourself saying, "Because I say so," a lot, it could be that you're bogging down in rules instead of principles. A rule implies punishment; if you think you're not going to get caught, then you have eliminated a major reason for obedience. A principle, on the other hand, can become an appendage, like a goal. It can become an integral part of the child, helping her define herself. "I am not a cheater," she says to herself. She may see other kids glancing at each other's tests, disobeying the rules, and maybe getting better grades. But they're cheaters. She's not obeying the rules. She's obeying herself.

Another good rule: "Brush your teeth before going to bed." This rule is even better if attached to a principle: **Keep yourself clean.** If the kid thinks of himself as a clean sort of person, he is more likely to keep up the good habit of tooth brushing and maybe even wash his own face by the time he's, oh, seventeen.

Other first-class principles: **Junk food makes you weak. The best things come with patience and work. The worst punishment for a bad deed is what it makes you think of yourself. When you fail something, learn something. Face up to bullies and your fears.**

THE THIRD PARENTAL PRINCIPLE:
Let Sleeping Babies Lie

DESPITE EVIDENCE TO THE CONTRARY, your child is a human being, a more or less autonomous and self-correcting entity. Even infants show an amazing ability to survive in a world that is not nearly as user-friendly as a mother's womb. This seemingly helpless creature knows at least as much as you do about child care: how much milk to suck, when it should sleep (not when *you* should, of course), whom to trust, and so on. The lesson for you is that *your child is not entirely yours.* She's on loan. She has a kind of autopilot that is already beginning to kick in, one that will be in overdrive in about fifteen years.

This is why children make terrible pets. Besides being enormously expensive and difficult to train (try making a four-year-old come to heel), kids really can't be owned. They go away when they grow up. Most parents eventually want them to. The hard part is understanding that all the preceding years are a process that prepares them to leave. The stages tend to be much more apparent at adolescence, a time when all parties may wish fervently for the separation. But children are getting ready to leave even at their cutest, most clinging stages.

If that thought bothers you—if you have children you'd love to keep around for a while—think instead how liberating it is not to own them. If your kids are helping to rear themselves, you're absolved of some guilt. You can *let them make their own mistakes.* Do they turn ankles on the sliding board? They're partly to blame! (Besides, a sore ankle is usually a less permanent injury than an acquired fear of risk.) A kid who thinks his parents will always catch him is in for a bad fall sooner or later. Then you're *really* talking about guilt.

This internal autopilot often controls the child's education more than school does and more than anything you can teach as a parent. World-renowned child psychologists look in awe as children blithely teach themselves without benefit of educational theories. Kids do the mental equivalent of push-ups, looking at the same book over and over and over, singing the same song until it's firmly embedded in *your* brain, taking apart valuable household equipment, exercising artistic license on walls and expensive books. Want to give a two-year-old educational toys for her birthday? Buy some cheap stuff at a yard sale and pack it lavishly in boxes and ribbons. The

---

Mother Liked Ezekiel Best

A FTER GRADUATING FROM COLLEGE and studying to be a lawyer, Daniel Webster turned down a lucrative government job that had been arranged by his father, Ebenezer. When Daniel came home and announced his decision, this is what his father said:

"Daniel, in the long struggle with poverty and adverse fortune that your mother and I have made to give you and Ezekiel an education, we have often talked over these sacrifices, and the prospects of our children. Your mother has often said to me that she had no fear about Ezekiel; that he had fixed and steady habits, and an indomitable energy. . . . But as for you, she did not know. Either you would be something or nothing, she did not know which. I think . . . you have fulfilled her prophecy. You have come to nothing."

Moral: Always take credit for your child's success. Hold yourself blameless for any failure. Ebenezer was right; at that point Daniel had come to nothing. Of course, when Dan eventually became the nation's leading constitutional lawyer and a member of Congress, Dad basked in the credit.

kid, who has not had the opportunity to read up on the latest studies of cognitive development, will invariably go for the packaging. *A toddler can teach you a lot about simple living.*

Not that you're entirely irrelevant, of course. You're a big influence on your offspring. But you can't determine how the kid turns out. That's *his* job. Think back to Chapter 3, where we talked about your inheritance of genes and family and personal experience. Think of your parents, and how they influenced you both genetically and educationally. They have a lot to do with how you turned out, but you're different in some ways from what they had expected or hoped. The same goes for your own parenting. *You can't expect your kids to be improved versions of yourself.* They just may turn out that way, but parents are usually the last to see it. If you want improvement, you just have to experiment on yourself. Your kids are sovereign territory.

THE FOURTH PARENTAL PRINCIPLE:
Story Time Is Better Than Private School

WHETHER OR NOT you provide your child with a blue-chip education, the single best way to make her grow up healthy, wealthy, and wise is to read a book to her every night before bed. If your schedule makes this impossible, set up a reading routine for a different time of the day, like early morning. Start a tradition at the earliest possible age, even before the child can talk. For most kids through the age of five the ritual— the snuggling, the reassuring sameness of the act—is even more important than the story. Every night put a few children's books on the bed, and leave the light on for a while. Good reading habits start before literacy. The act of holding a book, turning the pages, looking closely at the pictures segues right into reading the print.

This habit teaches an equally important one: the value of silence and solitude. Reading time can help recapture the family quietude that modernity has lost. In an essay, "Heating, Lighting, Plumbing, and Human Relations," in the journal *Landscape,* Albert Eide Parr speculates that the "era of candles and kerosene" helped foster close family ties. Lamps were too expensive to keep lit in every room, so activities were limited to a small space, mostly the living room. "Could it be pure accident that the generation gap does not seem to have been invented until after the invention of the electric light?" Parr asks. "Quiet, without complete silence, was naturally a condition particularly strongly insisted upon around the evening lamp, since you could close or turn your eyes, but not your ears."

Besides, books in bed create the cutest sight of all, a book lying like a tent over the face of a sleeping four-year-old, a scholar in the making.

Horace Never Did Learn Spinning, Though

HORACE GREELEY'S MOTHER was not known for her parenting skills; she was fond of the bottle and never could hold on to money. But she did practice one good habit with Horace and his four siblings: She read to them while she spun flax. As a result, the boy learned to read sideways and upside down, a useful skill for a printer and great newspaper editor.

Moral: If you just get story time right, you can compensate for a lot of mistakes.

THE FIFTH PARENTAL PRINCIPLE:
Sell the Call

WHEN THE UMP BEHIND THE PLATE sees a fastball whiz by the hitter somewhere between a strike and a ball, he yells, "STEEEEERIKE!" with more gusto than ever. The less sure he is, the more decisive he seems. He "sells the call."

An umpire should write a guide to child rearing. Manuals in the bookstores tell you that an essential trait of good parenting is consistency. The perfect parent always follows up a promise or a threat and issues the same judicial sentence to the same crime, every time. In other words, the ideal parent has a photographic memory, no emotions whatsoever, split-second reflexes, and a decisiveness that would earn a soldier a battlefield commission.

Aren't you sorry you're not the ideal parent?

Like the other two billion adults on this planet, you need a reasonable substitute for consistency when yours breaks down. You need to learn to sell the call.

All this means is that you must learn to act convincingly. Try hard to look sure of yourself when you discipline the kids, even when you're not. And take care never to contradict your spouse within earshot of the children. Think zone defense, not man-to-man.

How can you effect an unflappable demeanor when your child loudly demands a toy in a store at your most exhausted, harassed moment? Well, you probably can't. It helps to have had practice. Get in the habit of saying no properly when you aren't tired or harried (if you are lucky enough to have such moments around a kid). When conflict strikes, try for an appearance of disinterested objectivity, like a stern but fair judge. And remember:

THE SIXTH PARENTAL PRINCIPLE:
"No" Is Good Medicine

WHAT A STRIKE CALL IS TO AN UMPIRE, the word "no" is to a parent. Watch a baseball game during a disputed call; a batter who doesn't like a called strike often acts very like a young child. Unlike a professional baseball player, however, a kid benefits from a little negativity now and then. It is like the cod-liver oil of old, foul-tasting but healthful, and there is an additional moral benefit to the dosing. As a parent, "no" offers several opportunities for discipline:

+ It gives your child the ability to accept a loss. It takes practice to take failure and rejection with equanimity. When the parent says no with sufficient frequency when the question is relatively unimportant, the kid gets into the habit of controlling her emotions over the more important matters.

+ It sets comforting boundaries. Every kid wants a parent, whether she knows it or not. It's frightening being the leader of the pack at a tender age. Your saying no takes the leadership burden off the kid's shoulders.

+ It gives you the chance to punish whining or temper tantrums. The worse your kid's behavior, the harder you must sell the call. On the other hand, allow yourself to change your mind if the child uses a rational and convincing argument. At the very least, you prepare your kid for a prosperous career in the law.

+ It teaches the art of saying no properly. To a two-year-old, the word is magical, full of strange and wonderful powers. A toddler learns that a well-timed no can stop adults dead in their tracks. Your job as a parent is to teach a more sophisticated, less arbitrary use of the word. Whenever you say no, try to think of a principle to go with it. Are you denying the kid candy? Tell her that candy is not good for her and that she's had far too much of it lately. Does she want to balance on top of a high wall? Explain how difficult it would be to scrape her off the pavement. Your explanations need not be profound; you just want to get the kid used to hearing arguments associated with the word "no." If you can't think of a single reason why you have spontaneously denied your child something, well, you might just be wrong. Stick to your guns if the kid whines; be willing to change your mind in the face of his overwhelming logic.

➤ It makes the kid appreciate the times when you give in. Never say yes until the last possible moment; otherwise you could be in the embarrassing position of having reneged on a promise. (Kids who have not once remembered to close a door quietly somehow have total recall when it comes to promises.) Allow yourself to be persuaded. Cut a bargain. Say yes in exchange for a favor or a chore. Teach your kid the art of negotiating and the still nobler art of giving in properly. In any case, avoid power struggles. If your kid disobeys you after all, punish him for his sake, not your own. A saintly parent is one who can keep a stern face when she wants to laugh at a hilarious misdeed. She is saintly for her self-control and her sense of humor.

The ultimate lesson of good discipline is this: Although every child is smarter than her parents at some point in her life, her parents are always bound to be wiser. (This is not an unassailable fact of course, but hey, sell the call.)

These principles are easier to remember than to apply. That leads us to one of the most important principles to teach your children: It's all right to screw up. Parents do it all the time.

Jewels of Denial

+ When Jacques Cousteau was ten, his parents sent him to summer school at Lake Harvey, Vermont. He hated it. One of the most domineering teachers, a German named Mr. Boetz, made him ride horses. "I fell a lot," Cousteau recalled as an adult. "I still hate horses." Mr. Boetz also made him clean up the bottom of the lake under the springboard. "I worked very hard diving in that murk without goggles, without a mask, and that's where I learned to dive," Cousteau said. "I became a good swimmer. So that was the beginning."

+ Young Barbara Walters of Brookline, Massachusetts, also was denied the chance to go home after school. Instead she would take the MTA into Boston to her father's nightclub, the Latin Quarter, where she'd find a quiet spot to do her homework. She grew up able to concentrate easily in television newsrooms.

+ Bookish Vermonter George Perkins Marsh did little but read until he was seven, when his parents discovered his chronic eye trouble. His parents banished him from books for four years and forced him outside. He grew up to become the nation's first great conservation writer with his book *Man and Nature,* and he was hiking in the Alps in his late seventies.

+ Harriet Beecher Stowe's father forbade the reading of novels in his household. With a firm grounding in the Bible and philosophy, Harriet went on to write her generation's greatest indictment of slavery, *Uncle Tom's Cabin,* which also happened to be the best-selling novel of the century.

Moral: Denying a child what she wants can sometimes grant long-term wishes.

THE SEVENTH PARENTAL PRINCIPLE:
Don't Expect to Do Your Best

P ARENTING IS A DISTANCE EVENT, not a sprint. Nobody can go all out twenty-four hours a day. Therefore, it is important to think like a Puritan: your good grace should outweigh your regrettable behavior. If you fail to live up to your ideal image of a parent, then you have given your child the blessing of having a human being as a caregiver.

This is not to condone any abusive or neglectful behavior. There is no excuse for treating a child as a possession. Regardless of what the courts say, morally you don't own your kid. He owns himself. But suppose you love him and take pretty good care of him and still feel guilty that you're not the parent you want to be. You see other parents cooking fabulous meals, going on lovely Sunday outings, working skillfully on craft projects, coaching kids' sports, buying the best clothing and toys, sending them to private school. You don't have that kind of time and money.

Well, go ahead and feel guilty. It's good for you, keeps you on your toes. At the same time consider these two sources of absolution:

Sunday's Child

E ARLY IN THE eighteenth century, Israel Loring, a minister in Sudbury, Massachusetts, refused to baptize children who were born on the Sabbath. Puritans believed that anyone born on Sunday must have been wickedly conceived on Sunday. Then the Reverend Loring's own child was born on Sunday. He called in all the Sabbath-born children in the village and baptized them.

Moral: The ideal parent, if there is one, has the flexibility to make midcourse corrections.

1. Everything in your family is normal to your kids. They may compare you with other parents just because they see it gets a rise from you. But even if you don't do projects with your kids, they can still have a normal childhood. If you praise them, tell them you love them, yell at them for the best of reasons, and show yourself capable of forgiving and asking for forgiveness, your kids probably will have a better-than-normal childhood. They'll have a happy one.

2. Quality time is no substitute for quantity time. One of the greatest "activities" you can do with a seven-year-old is to lie together on a bed and stare at the ceiling. You may have the kind of kid who needs to be

---

But the Mare Might Have Suggested Whipping Them

I F DESPITE YOUR BEST EFFORTS, your kids still seem rotten, consider the saintly patience of Harvard tutor Henry Flynt. When he taught during the first half of the eighteenth century, the average age of a freshman was fifteen. It was a rare student who escaped fines for breaking windows, including Tutor Flynt's. One young charge put a live snake in the tutor's chamber; another cut the tail off his mare. After nearly every episode Tutor Flynt would rise in faculty meetings to argue for leniency. "Wild colts often make good horses," he would say.

Moral: It is easy in retrospect to see how the adult arose from the child. But it is impossible to predict the adult from the child beforehand. This should be a great comfort to every parent.

near exhaustion to hold still for very long. If so, start a bedtime ritual. Read from a book; then lie down for a while with the kid. Talk, or don't talk. Tickle, or just lie there. This is quantity time. If it seems a little boring, well, good.

One of the most important means of development is the childhood tradition of standing on a corner or in somebody's yard and saying, "What do you want to do?" The traditional response, of course, is "I don't know. What do *you* want to do?" Many overscheduled middle-class children are denied those exquisitely boring moments in which all life seems to be a rerun. Not only do periods of intense boredom teach a kid how to devise her own entertainment, but these empty moments also keep the kid from relying on others for her opinion of herself. Children don't need to be perpetually schooled. It's not natural. They need some downtime to school themselves. Boredom in a resourceful child is stimulating. And a good deal cheaper than ballet lessons.

EVERY DAY IS NOT CHILDREN'S DAY

ONE OF THE RITUALS of Mother's Day and Father's Day is the question that nearly every kid asks: "How come there isn't a Children's Day?" The only possible response, of course, is "Every day is Children's Day." The utter foolishness of this answer has failed to deter parents from giving it over the decades. The fact is, very few days are truly Children's Days. It is not easy to be a child, and what is more, kids rarely get a break from *being* kids, especially these days. Children are constantly being prepared for something; even their play tends to be purposeful and adult-supervised. Summer vacation can look a lot like school, what with camps or "recreational" programs.

Before the weekend was invented early in this century, holidays were much more common. The Sabbath was a day of leisure in America, with the rest of the week devoted to work. Celebrations were based around planting and the harvest. The Puritans did not celebrate Christmas; up until 1681 they outlawed it, considering it a pagan ritual falsely grafted onto Christianity. But they more than compensated with other holidays. They held Thanksgiving feasts whenever they felt like it, and they didn't stint on the food and drink.

The current American Thanksgiving festival has little in common with the Puritans' harvest festival, which they held in October, not November. We eat turkey and watch football. Families often come together at this time, and eating makes a wonderful ritual. But why not be like the Puritans and give thanks at other times of year as well? You could mark out a whole calendar of holidays simply by asking your kids what they're thankful for. Are they grateful that school doesn't last the year round? Why not celebrate the end of school? Toward the end of summer some kids are actually glad to go back to school. Hold a First Day of School Eve celebration. Consider honoring dates associated with family history: when you bought your house or when your grandparents became U.S. citizens. Go ahead and celebrate your wedding anniversary without the kids, but consider another celebration that includes them. In addition, try holidays associated with the seasons. The summer solstice, longest day of the year, is well worth celebrating. So is the winter solstice, when the days begin getting longer (after all, that's why Christmas is when it is). The first day of fishing season may deserve a holiday.

Small celebrations help focus the family, bringing you together for a common purpose. Little holidays also help take the pressure off big ones. Americans tell pollsters that Christmas is the most stressful time of the year. Americans make 40 percent of all their household purchases during the Christmas season, so there are budgetary stresses on top of all the other strains. We get mired in endless parties, eat and drink too much, and end up at the darkest time of year with a kind of holiday hangover. What is worse, our expectations for the holiday tend to be too high, and as you know, overly high expectations are anathema to simple living.

Maybe we're doing too much with too few holidays. Maybe we need to spread out our celebrating and do them all in a lower key.

THE EFFICIENT HOLIDAY

HOLIDAYS HAVE TO BE DONE PROPERLY in order to be simple. You must be efficient. The best way to explain this method of celebrating is to show a few examples.

+ **The caroling circuit.** Make the most of the winter holidays while expending the least effort. List all your friends within a twenty-minute drive. On a weekend afternoon, pack the car with hot chocolate, cookies, and little gifts if you want. Coax your kids or a couple of your most extroverted friends to come along. Drive to one friend's place and start singing. When the door opens, hand over paper cups of cocoa, a bag of cookies, and the gifts. Refuse to go inside unless you have time. Sing three songs. Leave for the next friend's home. You can easily hit eight families in two hours this way, without having a single muddy boot inside your house. Most local bookstores sell books of holiday carols; if you have a home computer, you can buy an inexpensive disk with lots of sheet music. Sometimes kids can borrow carol books from school or church.

There is no need to limit this neighborly event to the winter. Try doing it in the spring, with just about any repertoire you want: top forty hits, joke songs, camp songs, folk songs, work songs, anything that requires little teaching or sheet music. Caroling is too good an idea to limit to the traditional holiday season. Besides, at other times of the year you don't have to worry about keeping warm.

An ideal occasion for caroling, if your community hasn't left for vacation, is Fourth of July Eve. Sing patriotic songs; bring cookies and punch or sodas; give out paper Uncle Sam hats and little American flags. Kazoos make superb accompaniment.

✦ **A picking rendezvous.** Here is a great summer solstice (June 22) ritual: Invite friends to meet for a picking party at a farm within a forty-five-minute drive from town. Look up "Farm" and "Berry" in the yellow pages for prospects. Scope out the place before you invite anyone, and send directions with the invitations. Pack a picnic. Strawberries make ideal picking. Most farms will let you eat all you want without paying, provided you buy a box or two to take home. Blueberries are also good picking if you live in a region that grows them. Make room in your freezer before you go. Blueberries will last the winter in plastic freezer bags; just wash and drain the berries, and throw them into the bags. During a miserable stretch of winter take a bag out of the freezer before you go to bed. Put the berries on your cereal for breakfast for a bit of summery consolation. (Bags of frozen blueberries also make great holiday gifts. Just grab one out of the freezer, wrap it in aluminum foil and a bit of ribbon, and hand it to a friend who is bound to be grateful that it's fruit and not fruitcake.)

✦ **Motel pool party.** If you live in the North Country, try celebrating mud season. In late March and early April the snow melts, dirt roads turn to muck, fields become lakes, and a grim rain seems to fall ceaselessly. Cabin fever runs high. New Englanders enjoy boasting about the depth of the muck on their road and compare notes about years when it *really* rained.

If you aren't blessed with mud season in your part of the country, you can still celebrate. Find a motel with an indoor pool. Bargain for a special party rate. Motels often cater food at a reasonable price. If not, ask if you can bring your own. A few chains, such as Holiday Inn (800-365-3535), will set up the whole party for you. See if you can get special overnight group rates. That way, if you want alcohol for an adult party, nobody has to worry about driving.

✦ **Sports-TV party.** You can do this almost any time of year, not just Super Bowl Sunday, that great national football holiday in late January. Find a bar or restaurant that offers a wide selection of cable television, or call around and ask if a private room can't be provided with a big TV. Don't limit yourself to football. Consider organizing a party around televised synchronized swimming, a biathlon, or the Irish hurling championships. If no one knows the event, then everyone feels included. Borrow a book about the sport from the library so you can provide color commentary.

To keep costs down, arrange for a cash bar in which the guests pay for their own drinks. (Make sure you specify "cash bar" on the invitation.) You pay for the room and snacks.

✦ **Drive-in nostalgia.** Although the drive-in movie theater is dying out, chances are pretty good that there still is one within an hour's drive. For a wonderful end-of-summer party, invite friends to bring their cars, call the theater for that evening's show time, and plan to arrive an hour and a half early. Put blankets and pillows in the back of your car for comfort and small-child dozing. Pack a picnic dinner. Even the most video-jaded kids will be thrilled, and parents will find some pleasant (if secret) memories returning.

What do all these celebrations have in common? Not one of them is held in your house. The effort you expend is minimal. You maximize the number of people included, covering family and friends you may owe invitations to. You're being thoughtful, loving, and, best of all, efficient.

Note also that you have kept expenses low without being stingy. Being thoughtful does not necessarily mean spending a lot of money. This is a good principle to keep in mind as you read the next chapter.

CHAPTER 10

Weaning the Affections

*In which the reader discovers
the wealth that comes from shedding attachments*

T
HE PURITANS HAD NO OBJECTION to acquiring wealth, but they thought spending it was sinful. You were supposed to pursue your calling, not riches. On the other hand, *being* rich was okay. It was a sign that you were one of the elect, those who were favored by God. This is the Protestant work ethic in a nutshell: Get rich, but don't spend it.

Being human, many New Englanders forgot the second part of the ethic and spent their fortunes wildly. But frugality has remained one of the enduring Yankee traits, and you can see evidence of it right down to modern times. In 1968 Vermonter George Aiken spent $17.09 on his successful bid for reelection to the U.S. Senate. A lot of people voted for him because of how little he spent. But Vermonters are pikers compared with their neighbors

Paragons of Frugality

✦ Boston installed streetlamps shortly before the Revolution. The city saved oil by leaving them unlit when the moon was bright.

✦ When members of the Trinity Episcopal Church in Hartford needed money to restore their organ in 1990, they found the answer had fallen from heaven. Pigeons had left a century's worth of droppings in the church bell tower. Enterprising church members organized the Pigeon Poop Brigade, packaged the guano as fertilizer, and sold it for a dollar a pound.

✦ Lydia Maria Child, author of the 1829 book *The Frugal Housewife*, recommended earwax as the most practical cure for chapped lips.

✦ In 1925 Calvin Coolidge cut the White House budget by replacing paper cups with glasses, ordering that all manila envelopes be reused, rationing food, and reducing the number of towels.

✦ During the mid-1700s John Phillips was the wealthiest man in Exeter, New Hampshire. He soaked the backlog in his fireplace every night to save wood. When he entertained clergy, he served cheap wine; only the minister who was to preach the next day got a decent vintage. During family prayers he would put out the candle. It's not needed when your eyes are closed, he explained.

✦ Author John Mitchell wrote in *Yankee®* magazine about a Vermonter named Porter who was "the most frugal man I ever knew." Porter lived in a makeshift cabin and used dogs to keep him warm. Total annual energy bill: one hundred to two hundred dollars, "mostly for dog food."

Moral: The Puritans believed they were blessed with frugality as a sign of being saved. Today New Englanders believe blessings come from saving.

across the river. The annual salary of New Hampshire legislators, $100, is the nation's lowest. The state has the smallest percentage of public-aid participants in the nation. It even sells its road kill to the highest bidder—or did before a rabies epidemic shut the project down a couple years ago.

People make a mistake when they think modern Yankees have inherited a miserly prohibition against the enjoyment of things. Actually the Puritans thought it was fine to obtain pleasure from worldly goods. They just thought it a sin to let enjoyment get in the way of a person's calling. People should live "with weaned affections," they said. Just as a toddler enjoys milk but could survive without it, so the Puritans tried to live as if they had been weaned from mere bodily pleasures.

This is not such a terrible notion when you think about it. To this day many New Englanders believe that if someone works merely to obtain pleasure, he is a slave to pleasure. In such a case, as Poor Richard put it, "He does not possess wealth; it possesses him." You can tell if your own wealth possesses you by setting fire to your house and listing what you regret losing. Nathaniel Hawthorne thought neighborhoods should be burned down after fifty years. Thoreau wrote approvingly of the Aztecs, who he said would set fire to all they had every year. But that's a pretty drastic step, and your insurance company would probably object. An alternative would be to move. Benjamin Franklin said that moving three times is equal to one fire. Besides all that gets damaged, you're forced to decide each time what to leave behind.

THE MOOT MOVE

YOU CAN TELL EXPERIENCED TRAVELERS by their luggage. A frequent flier travels lightly, taking just enough for the trip. A veteran backpacker does the same thing. Both shed excess baggage over the years.

Each trip is a kind of move, in which you decide what to take and what to leave behind. We can apply this same lesson to our home lives. We tend to overpack for the lifetime journey. It is useful to leave some things behind.

One way is to rent a big truck, load everything in it, drive around the block, and then move it back in. Get rid of everything you don't feel like loading. (Just think of the interesting comments your neighbors will make.)

Well, of course you won't take this advice. But when you read it, did a picture begin to form in your head of what you would put in the truck? Can you imagine what you would leave behind, give away, sell, or just toss?

You can call that a moot move. In law school students hold make-believe courtroom battles and call them moot court (presumably because "let's pretend court" doesn't sound quite lawyerly enough). We'll steal the idea and apply it to an ersatz move. Consider making a list, putting everything you have into the following categories:

- ✦ Necessities (things that sustain life as you know it)
- ✦ Sentimental objects (things that connect you to loved ones, living or dead, or that are important to your past)
- ✦ Objects that help you toward your goals
- ✦ Objects that make you happy
- ✦ Objects that weigh you down
- ✦ Stuff that you'd just as soon get rid of

If most of what you listed in the last category is the junk of other family members, you might want to consult them before pitching it. First list your own possessions. What did you name as "necessities"? Did you include a car? A stereo? What would someone have listed in the nineteenth century? Is your definition of "necessity" a lot broader than what sustains life? Of course you want to have more than the bare necessities. But that is what the other categories are for: the possessions that help you toward your goals or that just plain make you happy.

Thoreau pointed out that most creatures need just two things: food and, in most cases, shelter. Humans in northern climates also need clothing. Thoreau pointed out that most of the work we do goes toward the extras: gathering or buying more food than we need for strength; accumulating clothes for modesty or social position as well as for warmth; building shelters that do far more than keep the rain off. Thoreau once toyed with the notion of living inside one of the boxes that railroad workers used to store their tools. Just drill a couple of breathing holes and you have a snug home for free. (He did not say what the railroad company would think of this plan.)

Thoreau made a good point even if he never actually lived in a box. We don't need much in the way of material goods. *Everything else is either something we want or something we don't want.* The person who knows the difference knows how to live simply.

Good Thing He Didn't
Blow the Money on a Cruise

WHEN PAUL REVERE WAS IN HIS THIRTIES, he invested in his first personal extravagance, a luxury for a town-dwelling artisan who lived where he worked. The new possession was a horse.

Moral: Pleasure in a worldly good can lead to a calling.

ATTACHMENTS

W E KNOW WE HAVE TOO MANY DEMANDS on our time, income, energy, and loyalties. We often even know what to toss over the side if we could only bring ourselves to do it. But we can't bear to. The reason: *We're attached to these complications.* We identify ourselves too much with them. Consider these two scenarios:

Martin drives a sports car called a Testosterone (or something like that). Not only does it have a CD player and leather upholstery and an engine with power like it's on steroids, but Martin also looks great driving it. If he drove a less expensive car, with more affordable monthly payments, Martin wouldn't get a stomachache every time his credit card bills came in the mail. But he can't see himself in a cheap car anymore. He feels a lot more like *somebody,* the kind of person he wants to look like, when he drives the car.

Susan, a production manager at an ad agency, has two beautiful little girls. Both are in a good day care center, but she wishes she could stay at home with them. Actually she could. Her husband is a highly paid medical technician who has just been made supervisor. Between his raise and the money they would save on day care, she could quit her job without hurting their budget. Susan doesn't hate her work; she just finds it less inspiring than her younger daughter's drawings or her elder girl's attempts to read. The problem is, she's a *professional,* not a homemaker. Much as she would enjoy it, being a full-time mother would seem like a demotion. How would she answer the ubiquitous question, What do you do?

Both Martin and Susan are burdened with appendages that complicate their lives. Martin's is an overendowed car, and Susan's is a job she doesn't want or need. But because Martin's car helps define him as a person, removing it from his life—performing a carectomy, if you will—would be a painful operation. A jobectomy for Susan sounds similarly scary. So they both find themselves drifting away from their callings.

There is nothing wrong with liking your car, of course. Nor is it a sin to have a job and children at the same time. (For most parents the job is a necessity.) But Susan and Martin make a mistake when they allow themselves to be defined by job or car. Our calling comes from our roots and our preferences, not our titles and possessions.

When George Heinrichs (the son of this book's writer) was five, he went for a drive with his mother. They passed a sign in someone's yard. George, who couldn't read yet, asked what it said. "It says 'Estate Sale,'" his mother replied. "That's when someone dies and they sell what's left over."

George looked horrified. "You mean like their *teeth?*"

George hadn't yet reached an age when he identified people with their earthly goods. He had seen the remains of animals in the woods, so he knew what's left over after death. Maybe we all need to think a bit more like George. In fact, if you look at the requirements of a five-year-old, you can learn a lot about adult needs. The Compleat Kindergartner is:

Healthy
Physically comfortable
Interested
Loved
Secure
Challenged
Growing

And Virtue Is Cheaper
Than Orthodoxy

NE OF JOHN ADAMS'S favorite quotations came from a book called *The Independent Whig:* "There was virtue in the world before there was orthodoxy in it."

Moral: Fashion and other forms of orthodoxy often stray from virtue.

Could you do any better as an adult? It might be harder for you to meet all those criteria than to own the car of your dreams, but chances are the list itself is pretty complete. You can use it as a kind of litmus test for your possessions. If you own something that contributes to one or more of the criteria, keep it. If it does more harm than good to the list, consider pitching it.

Sort of makes you think differently about wealth, doesn't it?

HOW TO GET RICH

SURVEY ONCE ASKED a group of millionaires how they made their money. Most said they had never set out to be rich, though they certainly didn't mind the wealth. They had just carried out an idea or followed a passion that ended up making money. Every one of them talked about working hard, taking risks, and focusing on the goals they set for their businesses, all of which they clearly loved doing. The wealth just followed.

Remember the genius fellows in Chapter 3, the lucky people who got grants for doing what they would have done without the money? The millionaires in the survey created their own genius fellowships. Wealth was the icing on the career cake. They didn't set out to own things. They pursued their own happiness.

Money is not the sole means to wealth. It can help a whole lot, of course. For one thing, it lets you avoid making some decisions, such as what to give up to obtain your goals. But what if you're good at such decisions? Then you don't need as much money.

To acquire this skill of becoming wealthy without the money, follow these three principles of wealth:

1. Think of money as means to your ends, not as an end in itself.

2. Avoid possessions that can make you poor by burdening you with expenses that keep you from your goals.

3. Take "plot samples" of what comes in and goes out. This is a simple way of determining how you spend what wealth you have.

Becoming rich requires discipline and courage, whether you have money or not. If you don't want to work too hard at getting rich, then congratulate yourself for not working too hard. In which case, are you really that poor?

Imagine what you could do if you were rich. Now think of the parts of that imagined life you could accomplish without all the money. (Sure, we've already asked this any number of times, but a frugal Yankee never lets a principle go to waste.)

If you prefer, think more modestly: How much more money would it take to make you truly happy? There are two ways to gain the wherewithal: You could get hold of the extra money by earning it or inheriting it or by some other means, or you could get rid of expenses you don't need. This

She Took the Rags with the Riches

SHE WAS KNOWN as the Witch of Wall Street for her tattered black dress and her brilliant investments. Hetty Green inherited five million dollars from her family in Medford, Massachusetts, and increased it to a hundred million. She made a killing in the bond market but earned her greatest fame as America's worst miser. Her son, Edward, lost a leg to gangrene when Hetty refused to pay for a doctor. Both her children suffered from malnutrition. She forced her daughter, Sylvia, to become a nun to avoid a dowry. Mrs. Green herself lived in a slum and once spent hours looking in the street for a coin that Edward had lost. She died in 1916, paranoid and friendless.

Moral: Money and wealth are not the same thing.

second option makes us clench our teeth, but if we view it properly, we might actually find greater luxury in fewer possessions.

Fashion often spurs us to burden ourselves with excess goods. "I say, beware of all enterprises that require new clothes," said Thoreau, "and not rather a new wearer of clothes." Too often we spend money on things simply because we think they're valuable, not because we value them. People in Connecticut tell a story about a man who decided to get rid of his refrigerator. He put it out on his front yard with a sign saying FREE REFRIGERATOR. Two weeks went by without a response. So the man changed the sign to read: REFRIGERATOR $100. The next day it was stolen.

It is this kind of silly logic that makes us borrow money we don't have. If we can't afford something, we tend to value it all the more. Credit cards give us the means to let our reach exceed our financial grasp. Plastic allows us not only to complicate our lives but to mortgage them.

Increasing numbers of American couples work not just one or two jobs but even three or four, moonlighting frantically to pay for their "lifestyle." American incomes have indeed gone down over the past two decades, and making ends meet takes more than it used to. But in addition to working harder, maybe we need to think harder about the ends. The more we believe we have to own, the more we must work to afford it. The more we earn, the more we pay in taxes. The more we pay in taxes, the more we have to work to make up the difference. Some lifestyle.

> # Why Thoreau Never Took Out a Home-Equity Loan
>
> ---
>
> T HE COST OF A THING is the amount of what I call life which is required to be exchanged for it, immediately or in the long run.
>
> —HENRY DAVID THOREAU

As Thoreau taught us, one way to save money is never to earn it in the first place.

THE HOUSEHOLD PLOT SAMPLE

U P TO THIS POINT we have used the word "budget" sparingly. As the federal government has proved, budgets are somewhat overrated. They won't make you rich any more than counting calories will make you thin. More important than tracking the money you spend is knowing what you're spending it *for*—not just how much but why.

That is not to say that budgets are useless; as you saw in Chapter 3, data and simple living go very well together. Taking a cue from that chapter, consider taking an occasional plot sample of your finances.

A plot sample is not a budget, although it might look like one. Start out by listing categories of income: salaries, tips, gifts, freelance or moonlighting money, anything you sell. An easy way to determine total net income is to look at your tax forms from last year and revise them for this year. Come up with an estimated total for the year.

Now list all the major categories you spend money on, for example:

Taxes
Mortgage or rent
Car
Travel and entertainment
Vacation
Insurance
Food
Clothing
Education
Medical expenses
Charity
Gifts
Savings
Pocket money

Take the last three months' worth of credit card bills and other records, and divide them into the categories you created. If you really want to be accurate, you could carry around a little notebook and jot down every expense. But most people find that more trouble than it's worth.

You may want to refer again to last year's tax records in order to calculate some of the expenses, such as insurance, taxes, and medical bills.

Just divide the year's expenses by four. Also keep in mind any major expenditure that can crop up before or after your sample period.

Now add up the totals, and see where you are. If expenses exceed a quarter of your yearly income, don't panic. Remember that your calculations are not costing you money; you're just testing. Besides, if you haven't noticed a large increase in your credit card debt or a decrease in your savings, it might be that some unusual expense is contaminating your plot sample—say, an unanticipated medical bill, a big repair, or an appliance gone hooey. Of course this sort of thing happens all the time, and you may want to allow for unpleasant financial surprises. Look at each category. Are you spending more than you think the category warrants?

ZEROING IN

IF YOU WANT, you can create a budget to adjust the spending in various categories and, if necessary, to reduce spending overall. For some people, this step is a necessity. But budgets can be restrictive and inflexible; they're not good at anticipating changes in your job or household, and they make you feel like a sinner when you stray. Rather than rules, let's concentrate on goals instead. If you're spending more than you want in any category, set a goal for that category. Suppose, for instance, your travel and entertainment are getting out of hand. The family goes out to a restaurant once a week, and every couple of weeks you and your spouse take in a first-run movie. Set a goal of eating out less and going to fewer movies. To avoid self-pity, treat yourself at home. Buy a good bottle of wine once a week, or take home a nice steak; rent a video on the night you would have gone out for a movie.

The same principle works for other categories as well. Don't set specific amounts as your goal; amounts are targets. Simply spending less is a goal. Try to establish new habits. If you're spending too much before the holidays, make a list of gifts for each family member, and try not to buy anything on impulse. Or if you want to spend less money on clothing, create a wardrobe plan and establish priority items—new shoes before a new blouse, for example, or a decent belt before another tie.

Coolidge Admits a Failing

AFTER DECIDING NOT TO RUN FOR REELECTION in 1928, President Calvin Coolidge told a member of his Cabinet: "I know how to save money. All my training has been in that direction. The country is in a sound financial position. Perhaps the time has come when we ought to spend money. I do not feel that I am qualified to do that."

Moral: The secret of frugality is to know not just how to save money but also how to spend it.

One of the plot sample categories—savings—makes you feel better when you increase the amount "spent" on it. If the rest of the categories aren't too far out of whack, some people make savings their first expenditure when they get their paychecks. Many savings plans, such as a 401(k), automatically deduct money from your pay. It's like paying taxes to your own future. This is one of the less painful financial habits since you're less likely to miss money you never see. If your employer doesn't offer a tax-deferred savings plan, talk to your banker about savings plans that help you with the habit, if not the taxes.

After you have set goals and habits for the categories that seem to need the discipline, you can determine reasonable targets. Plan a date three months or so from now for your next plot sample, when you'll examine your next three-month period to see if your habits are working. Your standard of measurement should be the targets you set for yourself.

In Chapter 4 we talk about the artillery method of setting targets. Keep in mind that *the bigger the target, the easier it is to hit.* Set multiple standards, and a range of standards, for each financial goal.

For instance, take the goal of spending less money on entertainment, including the expenses of eating out. Set several targets to help you measure your next three-month plot sample:

+ Take a bag lunch to work at least twice a week instead of buying lunch.
+ Go out to dinner no more than four times a month.
+ Go out to the movies no more than twice a month.
+ Spend 20 percent less on entertainment than you did in the last plot sample.

Notice that only one of the targets has to do directly with the goal itself; spending less money. That is because your *habits* are what will take you to the goal. The targets help you see whether the habits you set are doable— whether they fit you and how well you adapt to them.

What if you exercise astonishing self-control over those next three months and hit each of the first three targets but still end up spending more on entertainment than you want? What if you find that your expenses are down 10 percent instead of 20? Now our other artillery principle kicks in: *A missed target is a source of information.* It's clear that those particular habits will not save as much money as you'd hoped. You can either settle for saving less in that category or step up the habits: Take a bag lunch to work four days a week; go out to dinner just twice a month.

The point is not to save as much money as you can over a three-month period. Your goals should be for the long term, for at least as long as your income remains the same. Your plot sample is just that, an experiment, not a test of your moral fortitude. Even if you miss every one of the targets, you can't say that the experiment failed (or that *you* did, for that matter). You either have to come up with better habits or have to set a goal that seems more closely attached to your calling. It helps to carry out a two-part experiment, one simply to measure expenses over the past three months and the other to measure expenses against targets over the next three months. The process entails at least two sessions of sorting through bills and tax records. You might try scheduling the first session for the time you do your taxes. Then just make sure you put records of all your expenses in the same place so you can find them three months later.

STEADY HABITS

WHEN THE EXPERIMENT ENDS, you are ready to reconsider your habits. Habits are much simpler than budgets, and, if you can establish them, far more effective. Here are some good ones:

Get advice. Consult books, friends who are better at money than you are, and videos on money. Make sure you know the basics of borrowing money, buying a house or car, the differences between stocks, bonds, cash, and other forms of investment. A librarian can help you find reference guides. Consider assigning yourself and your spouse a reading list. Stay reasonably current with the world of finance. This doesn't necessarily mean reading the stock listings in the paper; just keep up with the news on interest rates, real estate prices, how the economy is doing in general.

Not a borrower be. If you can possibly help it, never borrow money unless it gives you a financial advantage. When you take out a loan, you force your future to pay your present.

Pay off credit card debts before they start accruing interest. Credit card rates would get lenders thrown in jail for usury in old New England. If you find it impossible to meet your card debts in time, do plot sample exercises over several three-month periods, setting targets for getting expenses in line. If you simply cannot live on your current income, you've got problems that credit cards can't solve. You need to work on increasing your income or finding another place to live.

On the other hand, if credit card debt is the result of impulse buying, take a pair of scissors and slice up every card. It's an awful pain to live without plastic. But debt is far worse. Ask your bank about declining balance cards, which work like credit cards without the credit. For a small fee, the bank will give you a plastic card that draws directly against your account. You get statements instead of bills in the mail, and you can use the card only so long as there is money in the account.

Never shop without a list of what you will buy. Or if you're shopping simply for recreation, set a firm limit on what you will spend. If you like to treat yourself, treat yourself with little things. A new book or CD can give you a much cheaper thrill than a large-screen TV you don't need.

Make a monthly list of things you need to buy for yourself and your family. Set a date on your calendar for sitting down and composing the list. Sort the items in order of (a) barely necessary, (b) necessary, (c) deeply desired, and (d) best put off for another time. Include an estimate of cost for each item. If you find something on sale, the low price might let you give the item greater priority. But if it's not on the list at all, don't buy it.

If lists don't work for you, **put a piece of paper in your purse or wallet with the following questions on it.** Allow yourself to buy something only after you've read the paper. (If you're easily embarrassed, pretend to be consulting a shopping list.)

Here's what the paper should say:

- ✦ Does this purchase meet or violate a goal?
- ✦ Do I want this, or is it my craving talking?
- ✦ Can I get it cheaper? Or is the convenience worth the expense?
- ✦ What would I rather have? Could I have both?

This habit works only if you're a reasonably obedient person, the kind who would never walk against a "Don't Walk" signal. Otherwise you might get heartily sick of that piece of paper and rebel against it, with disastrous results.

PLANNING

ONCE YOU HAVE your financial present in some order, it is time to work on the future. It may seem strange to talk about planning *after* doing the budgeting stuff. But remember, you weren't budgeting, you were only testing. Now that you have a good indication of your habits and preferences, you can think more clearly about the future.

Too many financial experts talk about finances as if they were separate from the rest of your life. The problem with this approach is that it tends to make money dictate everything else: "I'll make as much money as I can, invest it cleverly,

> # He Didn't Save Much, Though
>
> ━━━◆◆◆━━━
>
> I WAS RICH, if not in money, in sunny hours and summer days, and spent them lavishly.
> —HENRY DAVID THOREAU

and then decide what to do with it when I have enough."

How do you know when you have "enough"? Do you set a certain dollar amount? A year when you'd like to retire? What do you do with that nest egg? What's retirement *for*? These questions lead to all the non-financial issues that we've been talking about. The purpose of a financial retreat should be not to figure out how to get as much money as possible. You just have to plan how to link finances with the goals you have set for your life. The big money decisions should come last, after you have decided on the desires that you can fulfill *without* money.

If it weren't for family obligations, you could live like Thoreau, a man whose first true act of simplicity was to commit himself to a life of chastity. You wouldn't have to move into a cabin in a woods (which, what with property taxes and the cost of lakefront property, seems like a luxury today). You could live on less than ten thousand dollars a year in a suburban efficiency apartment, taking public transportation, eating frugally, spending leisure time in the public library. But you've got kids, debts, responsibilities, other plans. You have the future to worry about.

Good Thing Twain Could Afford It

"THERE ARE TWO TIMES in a man's life when he should not speculate," wrote Mark Twain, "when he can't afford it, and when he can." He should know. He lost his entire fortune in a single bad investment.

Moral: Twain's joke proves a New England proverb: "If you want to know what a man is really like, take notice how he acts when he loses money."

We've all been told of the rewards of hoarding money early and investing it for years. A little money does grow astonishingly large if invested properly for a long enough time. But before you start sacrificing for your future, you and your partner should first decide what that future is. Treat yourself to a financial retreat.

The idea of spending precious money and vacation time planning your future may sound only slightly more attractive than, say, boot camp. The whole notion of finances may make you more than a little nervous and guilty. But a well-run financial retreat should help turn down the anxiety volume.

As we saw earlier in this chapter, the chief advantage of wealth is that it keeps you from having to make as many decisions about what to give up. The flip side of this truth is, the more easily you can make financial decisions, the less money you need. A financial retreat can help make the choices seem less like torture. The trick is in treating yourself. If you can af-

And He That Is Middle-Class Had Better Watch It

HE THAT IS RICH need not live sparingly, and he that can live sparingly need not be rich.

—POOR RICHARD

ford it, book a weekend in a local hotel, or drive to a bed-and-breakfast. Don't go so far that your weekend gets eaten up with travel. Choose a place where you can feel spoiled and luxuriant for a couple of days. Many hotel chains offer low weekend rates and even throw in meals. If you can't get away, prepare a retreat at home. (See the section in the Chapter 8 on retreats for couples.) If the weekend goes well, your finances will be better off for it.

PREPARING FOR THE RETREAT

Six months before the retreat, gain a passing knowledge of your income and expenses. You might do a couple of plot samples before retreating.

Two months before the retreat, book the hotel. One night is sufficient; two nights are more fun. Assign some preparatory tasks to yourself and your partner. If you know absolutely nothing about managing or investing money, borrow a couple of books from the library. Don't let just one of you be the family expert. The one who knows the least about finances should do the most reading. That way the retreat won't turn into a lecture on economics.

In addition to reading, you and your partner should individually ask these questions:

- What do I want to do twenty years from now? When can I expect to stop working? What will I do then?
- Where should we live when we both stop working?
- What big expenses can we expect to incur before we stop working? College? House?
- What do I dream of doing in the next ten years? How much money would it take?
- Do both of us want to work? What would it take for one of us to quit and stay home?
- How much money are we saving? Am I happy with how that fund is growing? What are the savings for?

You don't have to discuss your answers with your partner. That's what the retreat is for.

When you pack to leave, include any data you might want to bring along, anything that tells you how much money you make and how much you spend. Plot samples are ideal.

After all this preparation you would think the agenda would be long and complicated. But it needn't be. Set yourself three purposes for the retreat:

1. To establish a reasonable level for savings and establish habits to get you there

2. To agree on how your income should be earned, spent, and invested

3. To tone down the nervousness either of you feels when thinking about money

If you meet any of these three targets, the retreat will have been worthwhile. Since they are fairly simple, set a simple agenda. An example:

SAMPLE RETREAT AGENDA

First Day

2:00   Check into hotel.

2:30   Set goals. You should be comfortable during this discussion. Have it while on a walk, in a café, or in the privacy of your room. Discuss:

> ✦ What you want to leave behind when you die
> ✦ Your ideal old age
> ✦ Worst-case old age
> ✦ Big-ticket items in the next five, ten, twenty years

4:30   Take a break.

5:00   Set up plot samples. Decide on the spending categories you want to reduce or increase. Don't worry about getting precise numbers to add up. You'll have another shot at this discussion.

6:30   Have dinner.

8:30–   This is your business.
bedtime

Next Day

5:00–7:00 Go for a walk or run. Read the paper. Or sleep.

7:30   Have breakfast. Eat in the room if possible.

8:00   Work on savings estimates. How much should you aim at saving during each three-month period? Just establish the amount you need to meet your long-term goals. If the figure you come up with seems impossible to meet, don't worry. That's what the next session is for.

10:00   Take a break.

10:30   Goals, part two. Now is the time to scale down the goals you set at the beginning of the retreat. The trick is to find a happy medium between what you want to accomplish in the future and the amount you can comfortably stow away in the present.

Are your travel plans worth a lot of current sacrifice? Are your retirement ideas too grandiose? Do you need to pay every cent of your kids' college education?

12:00   Have lunch.

12:30   Set up plot samples. Make sure all your spending categories add up to your current income.

2:00   Consider careers and future income. Given what you spend and what you want, what kind of work do you need to earn it? Discuss the future. If you need to get home, do this part in the car.

3:30   Done!

Well, not entirely. Just two more tasks:

✦ You might need to come up with an investment plan. If you're new at this, create the best plan you can, using available guides. Then, if you can afford it, ask a personal finance adviser to look at your plan and make specific suggestions. It may be too expensive to ask an adviser to write the plan itself; instead ask only for a critique of what you've done.
✦ Set another period for plot samples to test your spending categories. Give yourself a couple of months to settle into your new spending habits. Then establish your three-month plot.

When should you hold another retreat? Every two or three years are about right, unless your financial situation changes dramatically. You don't need to retreat to set new spending targets or take plot samples. But if you think you should change your long-term goals, it is time for another retreat.

Once this hard part is done, you can settle down to the pleasure of earning the wealth you have decided upon. That is what the next chapter is about.

CHAPTER 11

Work

On the life of leisure, and how to live it profitably

THE CAREERS OF MODERN PROFESSIONALS would have been considered lives of leisure in former times. Up until the 1920s most people sweated for a living. A minority had the money and social position to keep them off the fields and shop floors. They spent their workdays attending meetings, writing memos, and traveling. In other words, they lived like the sort of people who fly business class today. People in earlier centuries worked just as hard as today's professionals, and travel was even less comfortable; but the gentlemen of old nonetheless called their careers leisure. That is because of the marvelous contrast between their lives and those of the common masses. A business meeting can seem grueling, but it's a piece of cake compared with wrestling a plow.

"A life of leisure and a life of laziness are two things," Ben Franklin liked to say. He was a leisurely man who worked like crazy.

Lures of a Happy Calling

➤ Daniel Webster's son Fletcher reported that Webster wrote the famous address dedicating Boston's Bunker Hill Monument while he was fishing for trout. Dad didn't catch much at the time, said Fletcher.

➤ Another great work arose out of fishing when Massachusetts naturalist Clarence Birdseye caught a lunker in Labrador. The air temperature was twenty below zero, and the moment Birdseye pulled the fish out it froze solid. Back in camp he threw his catch into a bucket of water, where it quickly revived. Birdseye figured that flash freezing might be a good way to preserve food. So in 1925 he put the first frozen food on the market. It happened to be fish.

Moral: The life of leisure doesn't fuss with separating work and play too finely.

If hardworking leisure sounds alien today, maybe it shouldn't. We might learn something from that noble attitude. How can we parlay our lives so that they are filled with useful work and still feel leisurely? The answer is to find work so fulfilling and enjoyable that we would do it even if we didn't need the paycheck. As Thoreau said, "If the laborer gets no more than the wages which his employer pays him, he is cheated, he cheats himself."

"So," the reader replies, "there really *are* career opportunities for a professional sunbather?"

Not that we know of (unless George Hamilton is nearing retirement). If you haven't inherited a fortune, the life of leisure you envision is an ideal that must be modified by the need to earn money. Think of what you like to do, and combine that vision with a real job. If you think that you are working for yourself and not just for your possessions or for your employer, then you are living the life of leisure, which, not so coincidentally, is also the simple life. Follow your calling, and you live simply.

On the other hand, if what you love to do is not what your employer wants you to do, your life and your job are at cross-purposes. You have rented yourself out, selling your time to someone else. Lunchtime is a good test of whether your life and your job get along. Do you watch the clock waiting for the break? What do you do during lunch? Is it something you wish you could be doing all day? That could hint at your calling.

A failure to do what you want to do during the workday leaves very little time for living your own life. If you count in the time it takes to get dressed for work and to commute, how much free time does that leave you? Free time is time to do what you want. If you do what you want during the workday, then you have a lot more "free" time. Otherwise you have to squeeze in everything fun or fulfilling in too little leftover time, which tends to be when you're the most tired.

As we saw in earlier chapters, our lives are complicated by all the stuff we have to do. They're also complicated by regret over what we don't get to do.

THE KINDERGARTEN CAREER

CONSIDER THE COMPLEAT KINDERGARTNER from the previous chapter, the one who is Healthy, Physically Comfortable, Interested, Loved, Secure, Challenged, and Growing. If we denied a kid any one of these elements for a happy life, we'd hear about it—probably from the kid. Yet we don't pack many of them into our own workdays except during those fleeting hours of "free time." Suppose you could choose a career that met most of those kindergarten characteristics. Here's how it might look. (For the sake of our jobs, let's skip the "loved" part. Your coworkers may think you're great, but romance complicates the workday.):

Healthy. Your work doesn't hurt you.

Physically comfortable. There is adequate light, maybe even from a window. You get to sit or stand pretty much as you please. The work has enough variety to allow you to change positions or activities once in a while.

Interested. You can measure this by how much the time flies.

Secure. You feel appreciated by your superiors, paid what you're worth, and in little risk of losing your job in the near future.

Challenged. Your tasks are varied and pleasingly difficult; there is satisfaction in overcoming the obstacles.

Growing. You feel as if you're paid to get an education; you can see your career advancing as you work.

What else could you possibly want from a career? Vast wealth? Travel? Prestige? Power over legions of adoring staff? The sense that you're doing the world some good? There is nothing wrong with any of these desires. But they don't lead to elemental happiness hour by hour as much as the characteristics of the Compleat Kindergartner.

A magnificent salary is hard to spend at the office. The Ferrari sits in the parking garage; the mansion is a commute away; the vacation on the Riviera is just a memory; the thousand-dollar Hong Kong suit is mostly hidden behind a desk.

Business travel can be great—in moderation. Too much of it complicates life and wreaks havoc with the physical comfort category.

It feels good to name a prestigious job when someone asks what you do for a living. If you can get the prestige along with the kindergarten traits, go for it. But how often do people ask what you do? Is that worth giving up any kindergarten happiness?

If power is a means to making your job interesting and challenging, then it is great kindergarten stuff. But pursuing power for its own sake can turn your work into warfare; you waste time battling over territory and playing office politics. Pursuit of power can also become addictive, causing atrophy in other parts of your life, such as family and health.

Then there's the desire to do the world some good. It is hard to argue against a career that helps people or the environment. But if altruism is your sole motivation, you may not be able to keep up the enthusiasm over the long term. You do best what you like to do, day by day and hour by hour, unless you are one of those rare souls whose ardor for the cause sustains them.

The Pay Isn't Great, but Look at the Benefits

IN WESTERN VERMONT live the two legendary Galick brothers, aged ninety-four and eighty-three. They are famous throughout the region for their ability to fix anything—trucks, bulldozers, you name it. They charge a dollar an hour, not having raised their price since the 1950s. They love to work, but they manage to get a nap in during the day. In warm weather they sleep sitting in truck seats fixed to their porch.

Moral: The best kind of career is one you would never retire from.

YOUR CALLING

YOU CAN BUY DOZENS OF BOOKS on choosing a career. Most offer excellent advice on everything but how to discover your calling. Your career and your calling should be inseparable. When you think about pursuing a new line of work, don't ask yourself what kind of job you'd like. Ask instead what kind of day you want to live. The exercises in Chapter 3 might have given you some hints. Below are some additional questions that might help:

> Describe a perfect day. Can you figure out a way to make money having that kind of day?

If your fantasy looks a lot like vacation, ask yourself whether you'd really like to live that way year-round. Do you most enjoy sitting at poolside and talking on the phone? Which is the bigger thrill, the pool or the phone? There are many careers, from travel agent to stockbroker, that let you talk to people. The swimming pool part is trickier. Is it the sunbathing or the sitting that most appeals? Would it help to relocate to a warmer climate?

Your fantasy may go in an entirely different direction, say, a fancy conference room with beautifully dressed businesspeople listening raptly to your presentation. Again, break down the elements of this fantasy. Are the beautiful suits really important to you? Or does the idea of sharing your ideas with a group thrill you more? Happiness may lie in a teaching career at, say, an adult learning center.

Maybe you find ecstasy in your garden. This hobby suggests many kinds of work, but beware, making a career out of a hobby is as risky as letting a vacation inspire a job. You need to ask yourself whether you'd want to garden all day, every day. An avocation doesn't always make a good vocation.

> What sorts of things give you energy? Working alone? Collaborating with a team? Reading? Partying? Getting something done? What sorts of things make you feel drained?

These questions come closest to the themes of Chapter 3. Your calling gives you energy; distractions from your calling drain you. When most people dream about the simple life, they tend to yearn for a life free of distractions. The question you need to ask is: Distractions from what?

You may have done a double take at the mention of partying. What does that have to do with simple living? You may find the answer when you break your favorite activities down into root desires. If you like to party, what is it that most turns you on? If it's meeting new people and laughing at jokes, consider a career in sales. If you prefer organizing the party to the party itself, consider careers that allow you to organize, such as restaurant or hotel management, or meeting management, or catering, or even the moving business.

The essential principle of career fantasizing is this: **Take your dream and break it down.** Analyze your fantasy, dissecting it into the elements of a real-life career.

> What do you like most to do during the day: Play video
> games? Read? Schmooze? Eat? Tinker? Talk on the phone?

Happiness in a particular job has less to do with profound life meaning than with kindergarten characteristics. If you have a passion for video games, break it down: Do you love making a computer do your bidding? You might look into a career that lets you use computers or write software. On the other hand, if the chief stimulation of a video game is not the computer but the fast pace of the game, consider fields where you can be especially competitive or where the phone rings a lot.

Break down everything you like to do. If eating is a passion, what is it that most appeals? The infinite variety of food, the company at the table, the preparation of a meal? If you pride yourself on your discrimination, you might consider a career that has nothing to do with food—quality control, for example. A tinkerer does not have to be a mechanic. People who like to mess around under their cars often make superior problem solvers in places like business consulting firms.

Hobbies don't always make good careers, but if you break your hobby down into root desires, they can lead you in unexpectedly rewarding directions.

> Do you drive friends nuts with your lists and schedules?
> Or are you chronically late for everything? In school did you
> pull brilliant all-nighters and enjoy them? Or do you like
> planning things carefully in advance?

In choosing a career, you need to know not just your desires but also your personality. How do you behave when you're *not* working? Chances are very good that your character won't change all that much when you start a job. What were your chief strengths as a student? Your greatest weaknesses? When you think of careers, consider not just what you want to do but how well you could perform the individual tasks. What line of work plays to your strengths and minimizes your failings?

A weakness in one kind of job can be a strength in another. The student who chronically does homework at the last minute might make a lousy wedding planner but a great TV news producer.

EARLY BLOOMERS SYNDROME

I T TAKES MATURITY to become an adult kindergartner. One should not succeed at too tender an age. Pity the poor prodigies who get top grades in high school and go on to Ivy League universities, where they continue to excel. They're used to being the best at everything, and so when it comes time to think about life after college, they aim for the top notch.

Early Bloomers

"FOR PRECOCITY SOME GREAT PRICE IS ALWAYS DEMANDED sooner or later in life," said Margaret Fuller, herself a prodigy who died young in a shipwreck.

Zerah Colburn proves her point. As a small boy he could solve the most complicated mathematical puzzles entirely in his head. In 1812, at the age of eight, he went with his father from Cabot, Vermont, to tour the nation and Europe and perform before the king of England. But his genius seemed linked to his youth; the older he got, the longer he took to do the math. Zerah stayed in Europe for ten years until his father died. His mother didn't recognize the young man when he returned to the family farm. Colburn drifted from teaching to the ministry to languages. He died an obscure and disappointed professor at Norwich University in Vermont.

Late Bloomers

✦ When Sarah J. Hale was almost forty and a widow with five children, a publisher asked her to edit the nation's first magazine for women, *Ladies' Magazine*. She had never had a career before, or supervised anyone, or even worked in an office. She took the job and retired at ninety.

✦ In 1815 sheriffs threw thirty-two-year-old Frederic Tudor into debtor's prison. His dream of exporting ice to the West Indies had gone bust during the War of 1812 shipping embargo. Tudor pawned his way out of prison, built an icehouse in Havana, and received a shipload of New England ice. He introduced the first cold drinks to Cuba. After successful sales in the West Indies he sold ice throughout the U.S. South and allowed the felicitous invention of the mint julep. By the age of fifty he was a rich man. A year later he was back in prison for debt, having lost his fortune in a risky coffee venture. It took him fourteen years to repay his creditors. He died fabulously wealthy at eighty near the end of the Civil War.

✦ During the 1760s Abel Buell got caught counterfeiting. Connecticut authorities cut off the tip of an ear, held it on his tongue for a while, and then replaced it on the ear, where it eventually grew back. They branded him on the forehead with the letter *C*, holding the hot metal to his skin until he could finish saying, "God save the king." The talented young printer (an eavesdropper, not his phony notes, gave him away) went on to be the first in the American colonies to cut and cast native type. In 1769 the Connecticut Assembly gave him a subsidy of one hundred pounds to start a type foundry in New Haven.

✦ In 1857 Clara Barton was unemployed at the age of thirty-six. A Republican, she had lost her job in the U.S. Patent Office when the Democrats came to power. She moved back home to Worcester County, Massachusetts, where she unhappily kept house for her father. Then war came, and she hit her stride, becoming the greatest battlefield nurse in history. At the age of seventy-seven she was still working in hospitals in Cuba, aiding soldiers during the Spanish-American War.

Moral: People who hit their stride late tend to keep on striding.

When they job hunt, you rarely hear them discuss what they like to do during the day. Instead you see most of them trying to live up to their Ivy League degrees by going after money, prestige, power, impressive altruism. It is hard to make plans to tend bar and write a novel when your class-mates are making a killing or saving the world. It is especially hard to tell your parents that you have no idea how their sacrifices for your education will pay off materially.

Which would you rather be: a fast-track Ivy League grad or the uned-ucated P. T. Barnum, who, broke and unemployed at the age of forty-six, founded the Greatest Show on Earth? If you haven't done any impressive work yet, consider yourself a late bloomer. Your potential is before you.

SO WHO NEEDS EDUCATION?

A CTUALLY THESE DAYS Barnum could have a rough time. The na-tion's wealth flows toward college-trained workers, whom econo-mists call the cognitive elite. Harvard economist and Labor Secretary Robert Reich calls these people symbolic analysts because they manipu-late words or numbers or images. They may work in finance, the com-munications industry, or the law. They are trained as accountants, managers, software analysts, lawyers, or journalists, but they all have one thing in common: education. Nearly all have higher degrees. If you aren't one of these people, your standard of living is likely to decline over the next few decades. The contrast has never been so stark between the edu-cated elite and the rest of the country.

Does that mean you should run out and enroll in night school? Not necessarily. First, consider these principles of career education:

1. If the classes seem worth taking in their own right, take them. Enjoyment is the most important criterion. If the courses sound like tor-ture, don't take them. You probably won't do well. Consider something that sounds like more fun; your calling probably lies in that direction.

Even with the Degree,
Jeremiah, You're Still Dummer

Iɴ 1703 Hᴀʀᴠᴀʀᴅ turned down Jeremiah Dummer for a job on the faculty because he was overqualified. He had become the first Harvard man to receive a Ph.D. from abroad. The college thought he had gotten a little above himself. Still unemployed two years later, Dummer returned to London and became a successful agent for the American colonies.

Moral: Pursue a broad education for its own sake, not for a job. If you need education for a job, get the minimum required.

2. Education is no substitute for experience. Avoid professional training if you could get the job you want without it. You'll hear people in technical professions complain that they don't have the precise knowledge they need to hit the ground running. Years later, when they are promoted to management positions, they bemoan their lack of communication skills and their ignorance of sociology, psychology, and history, information they would have gotten in a liberal arts college. That leads us to the next principle.

3. Get a broad education for the long haul; get the minimum specific training needed to land a job. Once you have a job, you may need more educational credentials for promotion. But companies will often pay at least part of the tuition.

The point is not whether you're thoroughly qualified for a job. The questions are, Do you like the job and can you get the offer?

People Who Forged
Their Own Education

✦ If you think you don't have time to get a broad education on top of all the other things you do, consider Elihu Burritt of Worcester, Massachusetts, famous as the Learned Blacksmith. Early in the nineteenth century he translated Longfellow into Sanskrit and learned more than forty languages. He studied at the forge and after work. Here is a passage from his diary, quoted in Van Wyck Brooks's *Flowering of New England:* "*Monday,* June 18, headache; forty pages Cuvier's Theory of the Earth, sixty-four pages French, eleven hours forging. *Tuesday,* sixty-five lines of Hebrew, thirty pages of French, ten pages Cuvier's Theory, eight lines Syriac, ten ditto Danish, ten ditto Bohemian, nine ditto Polish, fifteen names of stars, ten hours forging. *Wednesday,* twenty-five lines Hebrew, fifty pages of astronomy, eleven hours forging. *Thursday,* fifty-five lines Hebrew, eight ditto Syriac, eleven hours forging. *Friday,* unwell, twelve hours forging. . . ."

✦ One of America's first great generals was a plump bookseller named Henry Knox. He figured out how to move a hundred artillery pieces from captured Fort Ticonderoga to Boston, helping to drive out the British. Where did Knox learn his military science? From books.

Moral: You don't need to attend classes to be educated.

It is hard to convince a twenty-two-year-old of this, but a new college graduate's greatest resources are health, energy, and relative lack of commitments. There are few times in life when there is so much personal freedom (of course, only if the recent grad isn't buried in college loans). Too much focus on the future can waste these resources. Imagine a young woman who goes straight to graduate school after college, spends several years qualifying herself for a respectable profession, works like a slave to pay off her loans, and then gets married and acquires husband, kids, and mortgage. All that is fine if she loves grad school and her work. But if more schooling is just an unpleasant stepping-stone, then she is throwing away her youth, committing the unpardonable offense of failing to lounge on a beach.

THE SIMPLE JOB HUNT

E VENTUALLY, THOUGH, the beach gets old, and thoughts of wearing clothing every day and earning a real paycheck actually start to sound appealing. Don't worry about seeking employment. You're already employed, beginning what you hope will be a short-lived career as a job hunter.

The chief goal of a job hunt doesn't have to be a job. For a new career, your main quarry should be information. If you fail to land a position right away and can keep from starving in the meantime, your career may be better off in the long run. Your pocketbook may need a job, but a career needs contacts. To get them, look beyond your first job and hunt for a career. Remember the habits of grace, and employ the following eight techniques:

1. Research each prospective employer. Don't waste interview time asking questions that you could answer with a little advance research. An employer can tell when an interviewer has made the effort.

2. Fine-tune your résumé and letter to each company. Don't make many copies of one résumé. Rewrite it for each employer, making it look as though your entire life had destined you for a job there and there alone (as, for all you know, it has). This technique is much easier if you have access to a personal computer and a laser printer.

3. Show up early. If the prospective employer can see you right away, you get more face-to-face time. At the very least you're less likely to show up late, an unpardonable job-hunting sin.

4. Ask about salaries, qualifications, how an applicant can stand out from the crowd. Ask the interviewer about her own career, how she got where she is.

5. Ask each contact for new contacts. Whom else should you be talking to in the profession or industry? Ask each contact if you can use her name to call the others. That way you don't have to make what salespeople term a cold call, in which you telephone someone out of the blue. Instead you can say, "Ms. Fatcat suggested I call you."

6. Immediately after each interview write a thank-you note. Tailor it to the individual person, and mention some part of the interview, preferably something you learned. Keep the note short, and send it so it arrives just a day or two after the interview. You'd be amazed how few people write such notes. A good, prompt letter makes you stand out from the crowd. It worked for George Bush, after all.

7. Develop good files. Put in everything you know about each company

---

And If You Can't Get There, Sue

⟶►◄⟵

A STUDENT ONCE ASKED Daniel Webster whether the profession of law was full. He answered, "The lower storey is crowded but there is always plenty of room upstairs."

That was one of P. T. Barnum's favorite sayings.

Moral: Don't think about the odds when you look for a job. All you need is one opening.

and each person with whom you interview. Jot down notes right after each conversation, and place them in the appropriate folders. Write neatly, and organize everything. The better the files, the more useful they will be throughout your career.

8. Keep up your contacts. When you land a paying job, send a letter to everyone with whom you interviewed thanking them for their help and encouragement. Whenever you can find a legitimate excuse to talk to them, use it. As you get to know them better, put them on your card list during the holidays, or perhaps send them cards on their birthdays. Work to acquire new contacts. When you visit a different city, consider dropping in on other members of your profession or industry. This is cheaper than attending conventions and can make for a higher-quality contact.

These techniques work for almost every kind of job. And you don't have to be just out of school to hunt down a new career. Use the simple job hunt if you are switching careers, are going back to work after raising children, or have been laid off.

Once you're established in a career, don't miss the chance to help out a job seeker yourself. That person is a contact for you. Most successful employees have formed the good habit of developing and maintaining contacts at all levels.

"But that's unfair!" you say. "Jobs ought to go to the most qualified, not the ones with the best contacts." Well, what is it that qualifies someone for a particular job? Technical skills, education, organization, an ability to work hard and meet deadlines? Sure, all those things. But every job also entails being part of a community—a member of a profession, a worker among workers, a supervisor who must motivate workers. Someone who shows skill in making friends, in doing favors and asking for favors is valuable at every step of the organizational ladder. Does that person sound like a politician? Yes, indeed. But there are good politicians and bad politicians.

THE PROFESSIONAL

S UPPOSE YOU FINISHED THE HUNT and landed the job of your dreams. The next step is to wake up because the job of your dreams usually isn't. Your boss is a jerk, everybody in the organization spends more time protecting turf than getting the job done, the hours are long, and promised promotions don't come through. Even your chair is uncomfortable. Other than that, it's a good job.

It's time to simplify.

You have many good reasons to feel sorry for yourself. But ultimately you have to think like a Yankee, an outlook that does not include self-pity. It is a wasteful emotion. Worse, it is unprofessional.

The main difference between a true professional and nearly everyone else is that a professional focuses on goals, while everyone else does not. If something gets in the way of goals, there is a problem. If not, no problem. Who sets the goals? Your boss is supposed to (unless you're the boss). Higher-ups are supposed to determine the broader goals. If they don't, it's up to the peons. We'll get to how in a minute.

There are goals that you should set for yourself as well. A good place to start is the Compleat Kindergartner: healthy, physically comfortable, interested, secure, challenged, growing. If your job does not meet all these criteria, you need to fix it, or it's time to work on your résumé again. Your workplace goals should go well with your bosses' goals, or at least you should couch your own desires in terms of those higher goals.

You usually see territorial battles at work when people aren't inspired by a central purpose for the company or institution. If you and your fellow workers are doing something particularly innovative or high in quality, something that makes you stand out from the competition, then you have a *cause*. That is how Egyptians got other Egyptians to build the pyramids, according to archaeologists. Representatives of the pharaoh went into vil-

---

And He Hadn't Even Started
the Feature Presentation

I N 1911 AN EX-JUNK DEALER named Louis Mayer opened the Colonial Theater in Haverhill, Massachusetts, to show moving pictures. "The Colonial is the zenith of my ambition," he told the crowd. Thirteen years later he was the head of Metro-Goldwyn-Mayer, the nation's largest movie company.

Moral: The most successful people allow their ambitions to ratchet up.

---

lages and picked out strong young men to join the crew. No one is sure about the job incentives. The pay probably wasn't great. But once they got to the building site, the men found themselves engaged in the greatest act of their lives. There is every reason to believe that morale was okay. How many people get the chance to perform a living devotion for a visible god who happened to be the pharaoh? How many can be involved in building the largest, most impressive structure ever created up to that point? Sure, there might have been some backbiting among the bureaucrats at headquarters. But when people believe they are part of something larger, office battles seem exactly as petty as they are.

How do you establish a cause in your work? Unless you're in management, that may be impossible. But it is a rare organization that at some point hasn't stated a mission. Your job (if no one else has done it) is to accept that mission and attach relevant goals to it. Suppose you're a management trainee for a fast-food franchise that dishes out fat-laden, mass-produced garbage to ad-dazzled customers who sit in uncomfort-

Great Causes

◆ Late in the eighteenth century Timothy Dexter of Newburyport, Massachusetts, made a fortune and created a business legend by selling coals to Newcastle. The English coal region had been suffering a miners' strike. Dexter went on to sell bed-warming pans to the West Indies, where they were used as molasses ladles.

◆ George Flanders is the reigning king of beans. Founder and president of the Flanders Bean-Hole-Beans Company, Inc., of Pittsfield, New Hampshire, he has revived the New England institution of the bean hole supper. A legume version of the clambake, the beans are slowly baked on coals in a hole dug in the ground. Flanders's dinners attract as many as eight hundred people at a time. "The beans keep me young," he told *Yankee®* magazine.

◆ When James T. Fields was a clerk in a nineteenth-century Boston bookshop, he earned local fame by his ability to tell in advance which book a customer was going to request. Fields's shop became a hangout for Longfellow, Emerson, and Stowe. He went on to cofound one of the great publishing houses, Ticknor & Fields.

Moral: True professionals can find glory in the mundane.

able chairs and masticate to insipid piped-in music. What's the cause in *that?* Well, if you think your job actually hurts people, you might look for another line of work. But you can justify fast food by saying that it provides convenience to people who don't have time to cook, that it offers hot meals at a low price in a clean, safe setting. That's the mission. Your goal as management trainee? To learn how to make the place as efficient and clean—and profitable—as possible.

Why do you need goals when what you're really working for is a paycheck? Two reasons: First, goals are wonderful allies in office politics. They allow you to fight your battles as a loyal employee. They help you measure the accuracy of criticism of superiors. They keep you from going crazy.

Second, goals give you a chance to measure your own performance. They give you confidence when no one else around you seems to recognize your work. They help you to focus on what's important and to eliminate the white noise. In short, they simplify.

As previous chapters have shown, goals help you structure targets as yardsticks of your performance. Make sure your goals match any your superiors set for you. Consider even putting them in writing and giving the higher-ups a copy.

THE HABITUAL WORKER

A S YOU CERTAINLY KNOW BY NOW, you can't simplify without habits. It would be impossible to list here every habit you need for your particular job. You might want to seek out a mentor for that; find a colleague or coworker who seems to be doing especially well, and study that person's habits. Ask for some pointers. At the very least, even if you don't learn anything profound, you will have neatly flattered a rising star.

In the meantime, consider some general work habits to make your work life more leisurely:

Set weekly targets. Managers will often give you targets and deadlines. If not, you can set them for yourself. In fact, it isn't a bad idea to set specific targets on a monthly, weekly, or even daily basis. Some work experts call this time management. But time does perfectly well on its own, without your involvement. The hours would pass whether you supervised them or not. You don't manage time. You manage yourself.

Sum up. Before you leave work at the end of the day, write down what you want to accomplish the next day. When you arrive in the morning, go over your plan. It could consist of three or four tasks written in pencil on the back of an envelope, nothing fancy. Check off the tasks as you get them done. Each month go over your targets. Don't think you have to meet all of them (unless your boss says you do). Set broad and varied targets, as we suggest in Chapter 4. Congratulate yourself for meeting a high percentage of them. Your targets should have dates or numbers attached to them, so they can be specific and measurable. They should be geared toward your goals. Ultimately they should help show progress in your career.

Set your priorities. Do what's most important first, least important last. Avoid the temptation to put fun tasks first. Save "dessert" for last; consider your most pleasurable duties virtual breaks.

Bundle your tasks. If possible, set regular daily times for each task; then the tasks themselves become habitual. While you probably can't eliminate interruptions, avoid interrupting yourself. Turn purposefully from one task to another.

Hit the morning running. Establish the day's momentum early. Don't spend excessive time socializing when you arrive at work. Arrive fully alert and ready to get started, even if that means getting up earlier and making your own coffee. Supervisors tend to watch employees most closely in the morning; early diligence could improve your reputation. In most office situations, interruptions are fewest in the early morning. If you're not a morning person, devote your first hour to what you hate doing most. What the heck, you feel crummy anyway.

Use clock watching as a sign. If you find yourself following the time so closely that it creeps, turn the habit into an experiment. When do you watch the clock the most? If it's a particular time of day, such as the hour before a break, save a fun task for that time. If you tend to watch the clock during a particularly boring duty, see if you can't change your circumstances. If you can't pass the duty on to someone else, consider doing it differently. If you usually sit, stand, or vice versa. Every now and then skip the break. Just work through it. By disrupting your break habits, you can eliminate the clock-watching habit. On the other hand, if you do little *but* watch the clock, you might need to change jobs.

Compensate for homework. If you have to bring work home at night, try to save it for a time when your family doesn't especially want your company. Five o'clock in the morning is ideal, as we note in Chapter 6. Early homework can give you superb momentum when you arrive at the workplace. (It can also make the afternoon a trial, but no routine is perfect.) If you must work at night, do everything you can to be flexible in reverse: Leave work early occasionally to be with your family. Let your kid visit you in the workplace. It's no sin to let work slop over into homelife. Nor is it a sin to let homelife come into work occasionally. Both habits let you slip into a life of leisure.

Play politics. Some workers announce proudly that they have nothing to do with politics. They're wrong. They may ignore the politicking around them, but they're very much a part of it. Workers who politic badly feel out of touch, betrayed, and confused. Avoiding politics does not lead to simple working. On the other hand, you don't have to be slimy and manipulative to be good at workplace politics. You just have to remember your Aristotle.

Chapter 8 offers Aristotle's advice for arguing with your spouse. (Actually, the advice he gave was supposed to apply to the management of a democracy, but let's not quibble.) The same rhetorical principles are good for the workplace, whether you're the boss or a peon. Let's review those three Greek words again and apply them to your career.

Ethos, your reputation among the managers and other workers. Remember how we said a Boy Scout makes the best husband (when he grows up, that is)? The Boy Scout oath isn't a bad set of criteria for the ideal employee either. Pick from these qualities the ones that seem most important to you: trustworthy, loyal, helpful, friendly, courteous, kind, obedient, cheerful, thrifty, brave, clean, and reverent. It's interesting how these words aren't often used to describe trial lawyers or corporate moguls. Maybe that is why we don't feel too sorry for them when they fail. Remember, Aristotle listed "ethos" first among the essentials of good argument.

Pathos, your knowledge of coworkers' and bosses' needs and emotions. Never make a proposal at work in your own terms. Always make it in terms of the people you're pitching to. Don't suggest how a change might affect you; show how it will benefit *them*. If you don't like a decision, show how it will hurt the decision maker, not you. Whining is death to a worker's ethos.

Logos, words and logic that lead to a consensus. In a good consensus everyone wins. A memo or presentation is a form of argument. How well it works depends not just on your language but also on your reputation and your understanding of the organization's (and higher-ups') needs.

THE VIRTUAL MANAGER

S HOULD YOU WORRY about management techniques if you're not a manager? The fact is, you *are* a manager, responsible for at least two people, yourself and your boss. You can tell yourself what to do whenever you want. You need to be more subtle with your boss. Help him meet his own goals, and in a way you're managing him. If he's not a good manager, he needs you all the more.

If you can organize your job to take on more duties, do it. Even if your pay doesn't go up, if you're unrecognized for the extra work, the experience alone may be worth it. Go for duties that give you new skills and contacts. In the worst case, draw up a plan that gives you the résumé and contacts to qualify you for a different job—in another company, if necessary. Most successful careers are endless job searches, helping colleagues find jobs, using colleagues to meet new colleagues, using colleagues to find jobs of your own. Become good at this, and you are halfway to becoming a member of the cognitive elite, composed mostly of people with good contacts. If in addition you can persuade people, know your way around a computer (a skill that, as computers improve, is getting easier all the time), and have the right education, then you *are* a member of the cognitive elite. You have a good shot at a great salary. Even more important, you have an improved chance at living where you want, doing what you want, and possibly even working *when* you want. You aren't merely managing your time. You're managing your life. That (need we say it again?) is what living simply *is*.

But wait. What about the working-when-you-want part? Increasing numbers of professionals—in the investment business, law, publishing, and a myriad of other fields—are finding it less necessary to spend eight hours a day, forty hours a week in the office. It started when people got personal computers at their jobs. They worked on the computer and talked on the phone, tasks that could be performed at home if they got computers. Then came modems, devices that hooked their computers to the phone, allowing people to communicate by electronic mail and send files back and forth. Then came the laptop computer, and professionals could turn a plane seat into a private office (which, for lovers of mystery novels and other aerial diversions, was admittedly a mixed blessing). What people once predicted would be the most amazing result of computers—the paperless office, in which information is created and stored electronically—became an even more amazing concept, the officeless office. Increasing numbers of professionals are using technology to free them from offices. Instead of working at jobs, many of them work on projects, getting hired by a variety of companies for specific, limited tasks. They diversify their employers the way an investor diversifies a portfolio. If they lose a job, they're not unemployed; they're just *less* employed.

More important, they own their time. When the fishing is good, they fish. When the working is good, they work. They merge work and play. They lead the life of leisure.

EDUCATIONAL PLAY

M OST OF US still don't have the luxury to knock off work and fish when we want. But that shouldn't keep us from having a little fun during the workday. Play can be productive. Look at a little kid playing alone in a room, working out social relationships with dolls, learning engineering with blocks, developing a sense of power and self-worth by trashing the bedroom. All this is educational, as the toy makers like to tell us. Why don't we take a cue from kids and use playtime to practice some of the skills that come hardest to us? Why don't we play "job interview" after dinner? Or a rousing game of "office politics"?

Well, maybe not. But too few managers encourage playtime for their employees at work. If workers have to learn a new set of skills—say, a computer program or a fancy phone system—the standard way to teach them is to send them to a seminar or hire an expensive consultant. Consider playtime instead. Ask employees to spend some time messing around with the equipment (under some supervision, if the equipment is easy to break). Has a new spreadsheet program come into the office? Have a computer person devise a puzzle that the software can solve, and offer a prize for the first solution. If the new program is a fancy word processor with built-in graphics, encourage people to create cards for the holidays. A new copier? Hold a party with a contest for the most original (G-rated) photocopy art.

"Yeah, sure," the harassed reader thinks. "Try playing around with *my* deadlines." But even crunch times can be playful. If a lot of clerical work has to be done in a hurry, hold a mailing bee, or a copying bee, or a run-the-envelopes-through-the-envelope-machine bee. If people of all levels work together, and if you have some decent snacks, then you duplicate what the Puritans did: combine work and play, making work playful and play useful.

That's what retreats do, when work groups go off someplace and talk together about the job, making plans for the next year. Retreats work best when the official agenda covers no more than half the time allotted. The rest of the retreat should involve earnest goofing around, preferably as a whole group. A hike, a game, readings, anything that the skeptics won't shoot down as utterly hokey, qualifies as useful goofing.

In almost every workplace there once was a device that pulled people together, encouraged short, informal conversation, and injected a bit of playtime and rest into the workday. It became a part of office lore and tradition. It was called the watercooler. Now that water is sold in little bottles, people don't hang around coolers anymore. Many supervisors would consider that a good thing, yet they agonize over office morale. They hire consultants, hold touchy-feely encounter meetings, admonish employees over battles, fight turf battles themselves. Is *that* efficient? Maybe some of them should try a little playtime, finding substitutes for the watercooler. One of the best is the coloring poster. In some central location, put up a large black-and-white picture and some markers in various colors. This could be a good place for regular meetings. Instead of sitting around a table, take turns coloring. It's interesting how a bit of kindergarten can

Playful Work

✦ Goldbeater Ephraim Bull spent more time gardening than goldbeating, especially after he had moved from his native Boston to Concord, Massachusetts. He spent years in an unsuccessful attempt to cultivate a grape that would ripen in the short New England summer. Then he spent sixteen more years working on a single promising local vine. In 1840 he achieved success: the Concord grape, which ripened a full two weeks earlier than any other. He spent another five years testing the variety before showing his find to the Massachusetts Horticultural Society. It was an instant success, but Mr. Bull himself died poor. He is buried in Concord's Sleepy Hollow Cemetery with Henry David Thoreau, Bronson Alcott, Ralph Waldo Emerson, and Nathaniel Hawthorne. Mr. Bull's headstone reads: "He sowed—others reaped."

✦ Quick, who invented the steamboat? No, it wasn't Robert Fulton. It was Samuel Morey of Orford, New Hampshire. Morey patented twenty-one inventions, including a steam-driven roasting spit and a windmill water pump. In 1792 he could be seen tooling up and down the Connecticut River in his self-propelled boat. He patented it in 1795 and piloted it from Hartford, Connecticut, to New York at a rate of more than five miles an hour. He would have launched the first steamboat line had his chief financial backer not gone bankrupt. Instead, Fulton and his people won the money and glory by infringing on Morey's patents. Unshaken, Morey happily continued sailing his invention in Fairlee Pond (now Lake Morey) in Vermont, right up until the day the boat sank. It lies there still.

Moral: The greatest hobbies are a playful version of a person's calling.

put things in perspective. A lot can get said over some detailed work with a marker. Blocks can serve the same purpose, or those soothing little executive toys that people put on their desks.

Do these things seem childish, trivial, and demeaning? Then they should fit right in with most office squabbles.

It's funny how much time and money we spend trying to act like grown-ups when kids often demonstrate the most efficient ways to work. Have you noticed how much of simple living is playful?

CHAPTER 12

Improving the Moment

On well-disciplined pleasure

I T MAY SEEM STRANGE to talk about play in the middle of a book about Yankees and simple living. Did the early New Englanders play? Did the *Puritans* play? As a matter of fact they did, though admittedly the first Yankees were no barrel of laughs. The Puritans said it was okay to enjoy something so long as its purpose was not pure enjoyment. "The wine is from God, the Drunkard is from the Devil," preached Increase Mather. The point, our forebears believed, was not to pass time but to "improve it."

One of the wisest ways to improve your time is to devote some of it to play—rightly understood, of course. For the sake of this discussion we'll use a pretty broad definition. Play is the time we take to balance our routines, to rest, and to prepare ourselves for the next stage in our lives. To play properly is not to waste time but to improve the moment.

Thus Explaining Why There Were So Few Puritan Comedy Clubs

THE FIRST BOOK ON HUMOR published in America, titled *The Government and Improvement of Mirth According to the Laws of Christianity*, came out in Boston in 1707. The author, Benjamin Colman, approved of jokes and noted that even the Bible allowed them. But being a good Puritan, Colman condemned too much of a good thing. "The measure of mirth may be prodigal and intemperate," he said. "There is a mean to be kept in all things. No excess is innocent. Mirth may be immoderate in the degree of it. Excessive *loud* it sometimes is, and sometimes excessive *long*."

Moral: The Puritans had few punch lines but a good point. Too much of anything isn't fun.

REST NOTES

EVERY SIMPLIFIER KNOWS that too much of a good thing is bad. If any one part of your life starts taking over the others, you need to balance the parts.

You can see evidence of imbalance in the health clubs of downtown Boston and in nearly every other major American city, where a battle takes place during lunch hour. Groups of men confront one another with frightening intensity. Injuries are common. These aren't street gangs; they are lawyers "playing" basketball. Their idea of a break from anger and aggression billed hourly is to do the same things on a different court. Many such ambitious people work so hard that they don't know how to play at all.

They brag that they are workaholics, noble sufferers of America's most attractive disease. But how well do workaholics work their lives?

Many people have forgotten a skill they had mastered in infancy, the ability to rest.

The historical characters who went farthest in life knew when to put on the brakes. You can experiment in literal braking. If you drive fast to work, see what happens if you leave early one morning and take the slow lane. Do you feel more relaxed? You're putting on the brakes. Here are some other habits of braking:

> ## And He Can Do It with His Eyes Closed
>
> ◄►◄
>
> H E THAT CAN TAKE REST is greater than he that can take cities.
>
> —POOR RICHARD

Count yourself down. In Chapter 7 we mention a seconds-counting exercise that helps you measure your pace in life. A similar exercise works to slow you down. Count to ten by saying "one one thousand, two one thousand," and so on. Now count the same way while looking at the second hand on your clock or watch. If you find that you were originally counting faster than the seconds, set aside a few minutes in your daily schedule to slow yourself down to real time.

Take your pulse. Sometimes you can get your heart rate down just by tracking it. Measure your pulse in twenty-second intervals, making a little game of slowing the beats over three intervals. (It helps to be away from the phone and from curious coworkers.) An alternative is to buy or borrow a watch that measures your pulse; most sporting goods stores carry wrist monitors that also tell time. You'll learn what increases your rate and what makes it slow down. Does a coworker send it soaring? Do the two of you have problems that you need to work out? Or a budding romance maybe?

Before leaving for work in the morning, sit. Just sit for two minutes doing nothing. It's amazing how the frenetic pace doesn't seem so important while you sit there, if you can discipline yourself just to sit.

When you stop at a red light, practice relaxing. Let your shoulders get heavy. Breathe deeply, letting your stomach go in and out. Grip the steering wheel tightly, and then let go. Relax your face into a smile. Turn a beaming look of love for humanity on to the people in the next lane. Watch them grip their steering wheels more tightly.

Plan some breaks. If you keep a daily schedule, build in breaks, if only for a couple minutes at a time. Close your eyes. Put your head down. Breathe deeply and then shallowly and slowly. See if you can't slow your heart rate.

Catch a "Z" or two. There are few better ways to slow you down than naps. If you have a place at work where you can close the door and put your feet up, you can turn napping into the shortest vacation ever invented. Of course too much daytime snoozing interferes with nighttime sleep, and that defeats the purpose of a nap. If you find yourself dropping off into a deep sleep the moment you lie down during the day, you probably aren't getting enough at night. But a cat-nap of fifteen or twenty minutes, with closed eyes or light dozing,

At Least Reagan Slept in Private

⇒━●━⇐

DANIEL WEBSTER, in his older years, often liked a nap after lunch. He slept on a bench in Lafayette Square, across the street from the White House. "I have some talent for sleeping," he once bragged.

Moral: For lifelong energy, you have to know when to rest.

can reset your internal clock and keep it from racing. A nap can give you perspective on your day, the way a good vacation lends perspective to your life.

Naps get bad press in this country. Some critics blamed the Depression on Calvin Coolidge's snoozing. When people heard that Ronald Reagan napped, they declared him old, decrepit, and lazy. If he was any of these things, though, napping was not a symptom. It helped give him that famous calm demeanor. We all could look a lot worse.

THE PERFECT VACATION

MOST PEOPLE TRULY REST only once or twice a year, when they're on vacation. You often hear reasons why two weeks should be the minimum time off: "You need the first week just to relax. The second week is when you really start to enjoy yourself." This vacation axiom is usually true. You know you're getting into vacation mode when work seems distant and unimportant and you spend much of your time anticipating the next meal. It takes some skill to do vacation right. The goal should be to go back to work willingly, refreshed and restored and with a new perspective on what counts most in your life.

And how often does *that* happen to you?

The problem is that you probably live with other people, each with a different notion of what constitutes a proper vacation. You want nothing more than a rustic little cabin by a lake. Your spouse wants a city hotel room and a guide to every museum. Your kids want to spend vacation waiting in line for gut-spilling amusement rides. Unless you're the rare family that achieves vacation unanimity, or you can take separate vacations without regard for rumors of marital difficulty, it might be a struggle to get the battery-charging benefits of time off.

Moments Improved

+ At forty-six, when P. T. Barnum was bankrupt and his wife was ill, he took a vacation on Long Island, staying at the house of a farmer. During a walk on the beach his family came across a twelve-foot whale that had washed up onshore. Barnum shipped it to a museum he had once owned in New York. The animal was exhibited in a large refrigerator, and the venture made a profit. The museum managers gave him enough of the proceeds to pay for the entire four months of vacation.

+ In 1860 Milton Bradley's Springfield, Massachusetts, printing business was failing. One night a friend tried to cheer him up by playing him in an old English board game. Bradley got inspired to invent a game he could make with his own lithograph. The result was the Checkered Game of Life and a gaming dynasty. Players advanced on a checkerboard, using a spinner (dice and cards smacked of immoral gambling). The object was to reach "Happy Old Age" through clean living, avoiding "Ruin," "Disgrace," and "Suicide." It was the perfect game for a society still heavily influenced by Puritanism. Bradley sold forty thousand copies within a year. In 1960 the Milton Bradley Company put out an anniversary edition of the game. Its new goal: to become a millionaire.

+ Depressed and tired, Horace Greeley left his office at the New York *Tribune* to take his first vacation in almost two decades. He "relaxed" by sailing to Europe and sending back dispatches about life in England, Scotland, Ireland, France, Italy, Switzerland, and the Rhineland.

Moral: People who vacation the way they work are having the wrong vacation or their calling is so pronounced that they don't need the break.

But throughout this book you have asked yourself how to accomplish the seemingly impossible. How can you live like a millionaire without the money? How can you "retire" while still working? You know that achieving these goals is not easy. They take discipline and imagination as well as the ability to make decisions. So you are mentally prepared for one of the toughest questions of all: How can you gain the benefits of vacation without going on vacation?

He'd Be Impossible on a Cruise

WE COMBAT OBSTACLES in order to get repose and, when got, the repose is insupportable.

—HENRY ADAMS

Well, okay, *go* on vacation, especially if you've already promised your family a trip to Cape Cod or Disney World. But even the ideal vacation comes only once or twice a year. Its benefits wear off, sometimes as soon as you return to the work that has piled up while you were away. The greatest single gift you can take away from vacation is a set of skills to apply to the rest of the year. Can you build enough relaxation into ordinary life to make vacations more of a pleasant change in routine and less of an emergency procedure? One way may be to take frequent small "vacations" lasting as little as a few hours.

THE THREE-HOUR VACATION

A S WE MENTIONED in the "Helpmeets" chapter, there is no better way to atone for past thoughtlessness than a well-planned evening for your spouse. Fill a room in your house with flowers and votive candles. Ask friends to keep the kids for Saturday night. Order the best takeout dinner you can find, or cook up something in advance. Draw a bath with oil. Tell your lover to show up at a precise time. Have a glass of champagne by the tub. Lay out her clothing for the evening, and tell her to show up an hour later in the room you have arranged. Once there, dance to music on a borrowed boom box. The next morning make her breakfast. Have a gift waiting on her plate.

With a little imagination you can achieve some of the effect of a vacation without going away or taking two weeks off. You don't have to exclude the kids either. One enchanted winter evening rent the movie *South Pacific,* and turn up the heat in the room where the TV is. Wear bathing suits, and eat pineapple and takeout Chinese. Put little paper umbrellas in your drinks. Give beach toys to each kid.

One advantage that the three-hour vacation has over the regular kind is that expectations tend to be much lower, and you know how we feel about lowered expectations. If you give presents on top of the partying, you turn the occasion into an unexpected celebration and add a little perspective to all the other evenings.

A few hours are no substitute for a real vacation. But if you're like an increasing number of Americans, you find it difficult to take as much time off as you want. Instead of a long vacation once or twice a year, you take more frequent short holidays, built around long weekends.

Cotton Mather, Fun Guy

"LAUDABLE RECREATIONS may be used now and then," Cotton Mather allowed. "But, I beseech you, Let those Recreations be used for Sauce, but not for Meat."

THE THREE-DAY VACATION

I F YOU HAD A WHOLE MONTH OFF, you wouldn't have to make many decisions. You could fit almost everything in: a trip to the beach, visits to relatives, household repairs, naps, catch-up reading. A well-done long weekend, on the other hand, requires as much planning and self-control as does wealth without money. You have to set goals and targets for the proper long weekend. Here are three standard goals:

1. The weekend should give you some perspective on your life, making you less anxious about work.
2. It should relax you. A related target is to find yourself not cussing a red light on your way back to work.
3. It should give you benefits that are scarce in your ordinary life, such as intellectual stimulation, fresh air and exercise, time out from duties and chores, sleep, or guilt-free luxury.

If it is hard to meet all three goals in one weekend, take several long weekends in a year, focusing on one or two goals per weekend. To get what you want out of the three days, you might consider devoting the time to a single theme. Some examples:

The Romantic Weekend. A bed-and-breakfast, a little too much wine, and thou. Plan it right, and you don't have to leave home. Your kids may object to this, so it helps to have a children's weekend to make up for it later.

The Intellectual Weekend. Spend the time researching or just reading about a single topic, something that has always sparked your curiosity. Study a painting in your art museum; read about the artist, examine the influences, and talk to a curator about how the painting inspired other paintings. You can organize a whole weekend around a play or musical performance. Do you have tickets to a rock concert? Hold a seminar with a few friends, getting someone knowledgeable to play the band's albums and the music that influenced them.

The Couch Potato Weekend. Stock up on convenience food. Put a fresh battery in the remote control. Rent a stack of movies; hunt up the TV listings. Avoid films that smack of art or good taste. Buy trashy magazines, bubble bath, snacks. Stay up late; sleep late; ditch the phone; don't leave home. You should go back to work happy to get out of the house, having had a refreshing excess of a good thing.

The Cook's Tour. Make a map of the food you and your family most want to eat in the course of three days. Plan the entire long weekend around food festivals, restaurants, delis, coffee shops, and bakeries. Spend the following week eating raw vegetables and cereal for dinner. Or plan a follow-up weekend that we call:

The Self-Made Spa. If you belong to a health club, schedule two hours a day in it, interspersed with vigorous walks and long naps. (In some clubs you can bring the kids along cheaply.) If you exercise at home, borrow some fitness videos. Before the weekend begins, fix healthful meals that you can easily whip together or heat in your microwave. Give each other massages. Go to bed early, get up early.

Shunpiking. There are two ways to shunpike, or drive back roads and explore new territory: planned and unplanned. Planning a several-day driving trip ensures rooms in motels or spots in campgrounds and helps avoid arguments about where to go next. On the other hand, the unplanned trip lets you be spontaneous. An inexpensive compromise is the use of your home or a friend's house as a base. Explore during the day, and come back at night. Hit every diner within a forty-mile radius, or go from yard sale to yard sale or historic site to historic site, or combine all those themes, stopping at whatever seems interesting.

Overnight Tenting. There are few better ways to get a change of perspective than camping. A vacation from routine like nothing else, it makes you glad to go back to work, where already brewed coffee is just sitting there. If you have small children, you should gain some camping experience on your own before attempting an ambitious trip. Shop for local hiking guides that show trails with shelters. The Appalachian Trail, stretching twenty-two hundred miles from Georgia to Maine, is the most elaborate, with lean-tos every five to ten miles.

The Family Day Hike. Before you try an overnight, first master the daylong family hike. There is no simpler way to spend your family time— or more difficult, if you do it unwisely. Bring water (your kids will actually drink it if it's in a cool-looking plastic canteen), and pack lunch. Make sure you have a destination: a mountaintop, a stream, a pond, a meadow, a hawk's nest, an overlook, a rope swing, even an old stone wall or an abandoned piece of farm equipment. It's best to have a bunch of destinations, landmarks along the route that help measure progress. Try to invite friends for your kids; they hike better with their peers. Bring a collecting bag for interesting stones, pieces of bark, leaves you want to identify later, flowers you can press between the pages of a book, the scat if you don't watch your kids closely. Prepare diligently, avoid unrealistic expectations, and you just may have an entire family enjoying itself in the woods. Keep in mind that you may not all be enjoying the same things, though.

STAKING OUT FUN TIME

A FTER YOU TAKE CARE of all your obligations—work, community meetings, kids' sports and lessons—who has time to hike or to leave on long weekends? To reserve time for play, put it on the calendar before anything else gets scheduled.

If this notion sounds alien, consider the fact that you already book time off; your calendar comes with dates for major holidays. You just need to add some. Book the longer vacations. Then look for Fridays and Mondays that are free for the whole family. Lastly, mark two-day weekends that you want to reserve for particular activities. It's a good idea to plan a season at least a month before it starts, so that the dates don't get preempted. Plan summer, for example, by the end of April. If you have to book hotels or resorts, you should schedule even sooner.

Hold a meeting with the family to plan the next season. What does each member most want to do during those three months? One kid wants to go to a drive-in movie at least twice. The other wants to climb at least two mountains. Your spouse wants a two-day canoe trip, and you want a shopping trip at a big mall two hours south. If you're the listing sort, write down all the activities for each person. Eliminate anything that's impractical or prohibitively expensive. Calculate how much time you need to accomplish everything. Eliminate low-priority items. Then set aside the necessary weekends, evenings, or days off. Mark them on the calendar so you can turn down any intruding obligations. That way you keep the complications from overwhelming the simpler things.

Listing can help for those periods when it's hard to know what to do, such as mud season. Museum going, bowling, shopping trips, a short-term membership at an indoor swimming pool: Anything qualifies if it lets you take advantage of the time of year instead of suffering from it.

Such times require the greatest diligence and imagination to stay in physical shape. Your exercise options tend to shut down in miserable weather either because you can't get outside or because you just don't feel like driving through sleet and wind to the Y to go swimming. You want to curl up and sleep through the season.

Well, who doesn't? Hibernating is one option during the dark time of year. But there are others, as the next chapter shows.

CHAPTER 13

The Soul's Vessel

The body, and how to control it

T HERE WAS A TIME when people didn't think very much about their bodies unless they were sick. The Puritans believed that illness was a physical manifestation of sinfulness. Most doctors in early New England were ministers skilled in treating moral disease. People who kept themselves free of illness often grew impressively plump. This was a sign that God favored them with physical prosperity. To be plump was to be good-looking.

These days the opposite is true. If you want to be admired, you should combine driving greed with agonizing self-restraint. It is hard to imagine a more complicated way to live.

The splendid physiques you see in movies cost a lot, requiring dietitians, personal trainers, home weight-training equipment, and maybe a little surgical magic. And they demand time that people with steady jobs just don't have. If you're rich in hours and dollars, you, too, can have a Holly-wood body along with all the other millionaire goodies.

What? You're not rich? Well, then, congratulations. You have lowered expectations about your body. Who expects your normal citizen to have an eye-popping chest and abs of steel?

Fashion can skew our expectations. Sexy billboards that hawk underwear may make our contentment with our merely utilitarian bodies seem as if we're settling for less. The wealthy don't have to choose between fitness and their jobs and families. They can exercise at home, vacation in spas, and hire people to cook healthful meals. But as we have seen, you don't have to be a millionaire to be happy with your possessions. You just have to make decisions and then follow through with them. The same goes for your body. It may have seen better days, but you couldn't live without it.

A Fisher of Souls

IN THE EARLY 1700s a minister named Joseph Seccombe of Kingston, New Hampshire, wrote the first American book ever published on sport. An avid fisherman, the Reverend Seccombe railed against restrictions on outdoor pleasures as "Bigottry and Superstition." Besides, he said, a bit of brisk fun is good for you. "Recreation and Exercise are necessary for the better Support of the Body," he wrote. "And the Soul, during her Residence in the Flesh, must have Suspensions from her more abstracted and serious Pursuits."

Moral: Reverend Seccombe understood what many health faddists miss: A truly simple health plan is good for the soul.

BODY AND SOUL

ACTUALLY MANY EARLY NEW ENGLANDERS thought you *could* live without your body. To them it was just a vessel to hold the immortal soul. If you value the container more than the contents, they believed, you commit the sin of vanity, with alarming consequences for your soul. Philosophers in Europe and America once kept human skulls on their desks to remind them that their souls were more important than their bodies over the long haul. Talk about your ultimate health plan. It would make an interesting exercise video: a Puritan divine barking, "Give me ten searching looks to heaven! Eyes up, everybody! Don't forget to breathe!"

Okay, that's a ridiculous image. But we've seen exercise videos that don't come off much better.

If you think of your body as an important possession, but still just as a

---

Dying Art

IN THE EIGHTEENTH CENTURY the Andover Theological Seminary in Massachusetts required students to make coffins. The work reminded the students of their fleeting life on earth while earning good money for the seminary.

It's just like a Yankee to combine a heavenly lesson with an earthly profit.

Moral: Avoid the sin of vanity—of getting obsessed about your body—and you acquire an important attribute of the simple life.

possession, you can begin to separate your mortal cravings from those things you desire as a person. There are three basic goals to caring for this body of yours:

1. Good health. Illness or debility can vastly complicate life.

2. The ability to carry out the physical activities you want to do: climb stairs without gasping, play baseball with kids, go on a long bike ride, carry a pack.

3. Adequate personal appearance. You may not want to be repellent to the opposite sex or to yourself.

Of these three categories, looks seem the least important, yet we spend fortunes in time and money to take care of appearance first. If you had nothing to worry about but your body, a career of diet and exercise would be simple living. But your template for improving yourself physically should not be a hard body. It should be your *own* body, at its best.

Back in Chapter 4 we talked about the reasons why nearly all dieters fail and why a few succeed. Those who lose weight permanently don't try to become other people; instead they decide to *restore* themselves to their true health and appearance. Picture yourself in your mind. What do you look like? That picture may not be entirely accurate. It could be a bit out-of-date. People over the age of thirty tend to think of themselves as younger than they actually are. A graduate of Middlebury College once attended the wrong reunion. He showed up during alumni week and hung out with a group that, though strangely unfamiliar, looked his age. He had a great time until someone asked him his class and directed him to the other end of campus. There he found a group of balding, paunchy, middle-aged alumni. The worst part was he recognized them as his classmates. He left early.

Don't pity that guy; if your image of yourself is better than what you see in the mirror, you have the makings of a good diet and exercise plan.

Great Moments in Health

+ Sam Adams's newspaper, the Boston *Advertiser,* was too radical for most Bostonians. But people read the paper anyway because of its great practical advice. One of its more talked-about hints: changing babies' clothing regularly, despite the popular notion that clean linen might "rob Children of the nourishing juices."
+ In the fall of 1956 logger Barney Roberg was working alone in the woods near Patten, Maine, when a white pine tree he was cutting kicked back off the stump and pinned him, bleeding, to another tree. It was impossible to use his chain saw to cut the tree in such a way as to free himself. So he cut his leg off. Then he tied a tourniquet around the stump and crawled two miles to his jeep. Managing somehow to operate the gas and clutch pedals with only one foot, he drove himself out of the woods and found assistance. Eight weeks later he was back at work, driving a bulldozer. Roberg later recalled that the doctor in the hospital said the only chance he had for survival was to allow the removal of the rest of his leg above the knee. "Listen here, Doc," Roberg replied, "I done all the cutting on that leg that's going to be done. I got it trimmed up just the way I want it. Now you leave it alone."
+ The great eighteenth-century Harvard scientist Edward Augustus Holyoke warned against drinking "cold water or other weak small Liquids" after exercise without first downing a glass of rum. He ate lots of fruit, smoked two pipes a day, and on his hundredth birthday walked to a dinner given in his honor.

Moral: Good health includes a healthy dose of self-help.

YOU VERSUS YOUR CRAVINGS

THE BODY YOU SEE IN THE MIRROR is the result of genes, time, and habits. As you get farther from the age of twenty-five, either your habits must change or your body will. You can either decide not to mind or do something about it. That means changing your habits.

Option One: not minding. This may be the right choice for you. Does your lover seem happy with the way you are? Do you enjoy sports or walking or gardening without feeling crippled? Does your doctor seem unalarmed during a checkup? If health, abilities, and appearance are in good working order, then it just might not be worth changing your body. Your habits may be fine as they are, so why go to the trouble? The trick to simple living is not just to develop the right goals. First you have to know when to be satisfied.

Option Two: changing your habits. If your body is out of whack in any of the three categories, then you can exercise this option.

Before you start fixing, though, you need to know what's broke. If you are overweight, for example, you still need to know *how* you are overweight. Does a chart in a magazine say you weigh too much for your height? Don't believe it until you talk to a doctor. Without some knowledge of your medical history and genetic heritage, it's hard to say you weigh too much for good health unless you're truly obese, meaning 20 percent heavier than the charts say you should be. If you happen not to look like an underwear model, that doesn't mean you're unhealthy. Skinny isn't necessarily fit.

Are you disgusted with the way you look? Your appearance may not be the problem; talk to a medical professional or a member of the clergy about your feelings. No diet plan will cure you of a psychological or spiritual ailment.

Do you look like a stranger in the mirror? If you're convinced your weight is the reason, it still might be a good idea to talk to a close friend who can give you an honest assessment. Maybe you *do* weigh more than you should.

If you already have reasonable habits—if you don't overeat, if less than 20 percent of your diet is from fat, if you get half an hour's continual exercise at least three times a week and avoid consuming much alcohol—then chances are that your body is close to its natural state. The most successful diet plans, remember, are those that aim at bringing the body to this state. Call it your fate, and remember our oft-repeated moral that a well-chosen goal looks a lot like fate. (The obverse of this principle is

---

Couldn't He Just Settle for Makeup?

NATHANIEL HAWTHORNE wrote a short story, "The Birthmark," about a disastrous makeover. A great scientist marries a beautiful woman who is nearly flawless except for a tiny mark on her cheek. The doctor becomes obsessed with the spot, the only thing standing between the woman and perfection. He experiments on her night and day and finally creates a potion to get rid of the mark. But just as the spot disappears, the woman dies. Probably the scariest dermatology story ever written.

Moral: Although he probably didn't mean to, Hawthorne has written a cautionary tale for modern Americans who can't be satisfied with the bodies they (or their spouses) have.

that your fate, including your body's natural state, makes a good goal.) You could improve your body, of course. Cut the fat even more; avoid alcohol altogether; exercise longer, more vigorously, and more often. Your body could become an interesting hobby, a continuing physical experiment. Some people work on their cars or their gardens. You work on your body.

But if you feel ashamed because you don't follow these superhabits, you might work first on your shame, not on the habits. The first habits to change are those that cause your body to complicate your life. Dramatic diets and excessive workouts can be just as complicating as eating like a pig and living like a sloth.

While we're at it, though, let's get to the eating-like-a-pig part.

In a bit we'll talk more about goals and targets that can help you establish good habits and eliminate the bad ones. But first, let's list some larger principles. If you are what you eat, then a principled eater is . . . well, let's not get carried away. You may be surprised to find that much of the list is not very painful. Why should eating (or not eating) be a form of punishment? Excessive dieting does not simplify your life any more than excessive eating does.

In fact, as you'll see, we don't believe in dieting at all.

SIMPLE EATING PRINCIPLES
(A Baker's Dozen)

1. Don't diet. In the chapter "Weaning the Affections," we talked about budgeting and dieting being the same thing. The problem with both is that they tend to create goals that are too short and difficult. They aren't tied to lifetime habits. It is possible for a person who says, "I am on a diet," to lose some weight. But all the lost poundage usually comes back, and then some. There are two important reasons for the long-term failure of diets. One is that the very expression "I am on a diet" implies that it's temporary. If you're "on" a diet, then you probably intend to go "off" it at some point. You're fighting your body's natural tendency to stick to habits.

This leads to the second reason a diet almost always fails over the long run: Your body gets used to it. If you eat dramatically less, you might lose weight rapidly. But your system quickly adjusts to the new intake, using each calorie more efficiently. When you go off your diet, your body dutifully harbors the extra food as fat, at a greater rate than it did before you began your weight loss program. In other words, the less you eat, the better your body gets at converting calories to fat. It's a very fast learner, your body.

If you want to become a slimmer person, don't set short-term dietary goals. Establish permanent habits, and gradually reduce the amount you eat. Give your body time to get used to being thinner, and then you and it will be allies, not enemies.

2. Don't give up anything. Unless your doctor forbids certain foods, avoid painful taboos. Don't forswear ice cream, steak, french fries, or oysters. If you try to give them up entirely, you will feel like a failure when you eat them. Just don't consume as much. Eat smaller portions less often. Has it been weeks since you ate a steak in a restaurant? Go ahead and order the steak. But don't get the kind that fills up a large plate, or if you do, cut it in half and immediately ask for a doggie bag. An occasional ice-cream cone isn't bad for you. But order one scoop; two aren't twice as enjoyable. And don't make going out for ice cream a habit. That ruins it as a treat.

3. Don't just eat "lite." Many people attempt to lose weight by relying on processed foods with reduced fat and calories. There is nothing inherently wrong with these foods, but studies show that consumers who buy them tend to eat more of these foods than they would if the fat were left

The First Fad Diet Ever

TALK ABOUT DIGESTING THINGS to their essence. New Hampshirite Horace Fletcher elevated chewing to a virtue in two best-selling books. A painter, journalist, and shipping magnate, Fletcher flunked a medical exam for life insurance in 1895. Determined to lose fifty pounds and to cure his chronic indigestion, he discovered the mealtime secret to happiness and well-being: chewing every mouthful until the food "swallows itself." He described this principle in his books, *Menticulture, or The A-B-C of True Living* and *Happiness as Found in Forethought Minus Fear-thought.* "To fletcherize" became an expression known to every well-masticating household. Among his most famous adherents was the ruminative novelist Henry James.

The cure worked for Fletcher himself as well—he celebrated his fiftieth birthday by riding almost two hundred miles on a bicycle—but it didn't work perfectly. He died at the age of sixty of bronchitis.

If you're trying to limit the amount you eat, consider following the esophageal ethic of Horace Fletcher, who chewed one hundred times before every swallow. At the very least you will eat less between meals. You won't have time.

Moral: Don't fall for diets. Fall into habits.

in. The result: larger portions of less-satisfying food, no savings in calories, no lost weight.

It's good to cut some fat out of your diet. Researchers now say that a 20 percent fat content is healthy; the average for Americans is twice that amount. But if you cut out the fat without also reducing the *amount* you eat, you may not be helping yourself. Instead of limiting what you eat, limit how much. You eventually should find yourself feeling full with less food. Your body adjusts more easily to smaller amounts of food than to limitations on the types of foods you eat. Eat as varied a diet as you can, limit the fat-laden dishes to occasional treats, and eat less overall. You'll get slimmer and avoid self-pity.

4. Plan to eat in excess. Now and then you just have to cut loose. That's what this principle is for. As you know by now, a central concept in simple living is to do nothing to excess, including the excessive avoidance of excess. An overly restrictive life can be complicated and doomed to failure. Don't attempt to eliminate all your vices. Corral them instead. Limit ice cream to the weekend, for example. (That's a good system for alcohol as well. Don't have more than two drinks in a day, and drink only on Friday and Saturday nights.)

Another technique is to binge on the holidays. Don't stint on the gravy and pie on Thanksgiving. Pig out at New Year's. Eat all you want on your birthday, guilt-free. What's the sin in celebrating? The Puritans did it like gangbusters. But don't just binge; *use* the bingeing as a way to eliminate self-pity. Have you chosen to cut way back on pie? Give yourself a pie-eating time to look forward to. Treat it as a kind of food vacation, when you let your dietary hair down. The rest of the time you have to get real. So what if you gain a pound or two over the holidays? You planned to all along.

Nearly everyone strays from good eating. But you don't have to lose control; just *plan* to stray, and use your eating holidays to keep from straying the rest of the time.

5. Eat *really* fast food. Not only are most fast-food meals terrible for you, but they're not always that fast. You have to drive to the restaurant, wait in line, give your order, pay, discover that your order is incomplete, go back and try again. Sure, it's still probably faster than if you went out for a sit-down meal with table service. But if you tend to go out for lunch at work, consider this alternative: Pack a lunch of fruit, a hunk of good unsliced bread, and a can of fruit juice. You may have to peel an orange or banana, but that's it. You don't have to wait in line, heat anything up, or even spend much time packing in the morning.

6. Snack between meals. If this principle seems surprising, consider that *when* you eat isn't as important as *what* you eat and how much. Your body lays on less fat if it's never too hungry or too glutted. If you eat some fruit now and then—especially around three o'clock in the afternoon, when your body's blood sugar tends to be at its lowest level and energy may be flagging—you might eat less at mealtime, and there may be less temptation to eat chips or candy for an energy boost.

7. Cook in bulk. Create your own fast food and snacks by preparing them once or twice a week. Cook a large amount of pasta shells or macaroni, for example, and keep it in the fridge. Buy different sauces to go with it, along with cottage cheese and oil and vegetables for pasta salad. Keep a large bowl full of as many different kinds of fruit as you can find in season. Save small paper bags when you go shopping, and reuse them as lunch bags. Buy dried fruit for snacks at work.

8. Eat a Puritan dinner. If you can swing it, make midday your big mealtime, as our forebears did. Pack some hot soup or stew in a thermos with lunch. Then eat light for supper: salad, fruit, milk and cereal if you like, or a baked potato hot out of the microwave. You're less likely to put on weight if you don't go to bed full. Besides, a light supper is easier to prepare after a day of work.

> ## Chocolate Being an Exception
>
> ⇌⇌●⇌⇌
>
> Eat to live, and not live to eat.
> —POOR RICHARD

9. Give thanks for your food. Why is saying grace a good eating habit? Besides being one of the most common ways for families to worship on a daily basis, a mealtime blessing makes you more conscious of what you're eating. Consider naming the food as you give thanks for it. Don't just consume; partake. If your eating habits are bad, one reason could be that they are unconscious; you take food for granted. A little ceremony before you eat could make you more aware of eating.

10. Eat slowly. Follow Horace Fletcher's advice (see the sidebar on page 215), and chew each bite. Establish chewing as a habit, and you may not have time to eat as much as you used to.

11. Eat until you're not hungry. Our worst dietary practices have to do with extremes. We eat beyond hunger, then periodically starve ourselves with diet plans. Instead we should learn to let our bodies tell us when to stop eating.

Most babies know this art better than adults do. Breast-feeding infants take in exactly what they need. They have the simplest diets of all: no complicated choices, extremely fast food (a few screams, and boom! there it is), and no anorexic models to compare themselves with.

We adult humans can adapt this same principle—or "infant formula," if you will. Eat when you're hungry. Stop eating when you're not hungry. If you stick mostly to the foods that are good for you, avoiding too much fat and sugar, then your body will take what it needs and will tell you when to stop. The long-term result, if you exercise properly, will be the weight you're supposed to be.

12. Eat for after the meal. Conduct a little cost-benefit analysis before you eat something. Will you be glad you ate this food an hour from now? A day from now?

You don't have to regret eating a candy bar. If you're sure you will enjoy it, go ahead and eat it. But if fat and calories will outweigh the pleasure an hour after you've swallowed it, the candy bar may not seem worth it. The pleasure should outweigh the pain, including the painful regrets.

13. Treat yourself; don't reward yourself. When you eat something that isn't good for your body, do it for the pleasure, not as a reward for some good deed you did. If you use junk food as a bribe, you risk inflation, giving yourself bigger rewards for less effort. You want an ice-cream cone? Go ahead, as long as the pleasure outweighs the pain. Don't do it because you've gone for a run. Exercise, like eating, should be done for its own rewards.

CHAIRMAN MAO'S REVOLUTIONARY WEIGHT LOSS PLAN

YOU MAY FIND DIETING far removed from the subject of the Chinese Revolution. True, Mao Zedong doesn't seem to have worried much about overeating. He lived in a country where the point was to get enough to eat, not how to burn it off again. (In fact, he is accused of fomenting mass starvation.)

Nonetheless, you can apply Mao's strategic wisdom to various aspects of your own life. When Henry Kissinger was a Harvard professor, he admired the Chinese Communists for this principle: **Once you set a goal, stick to the goal, not necessarily to the details of the plan.** Mao went into each battle expecting to win. When he lost, which happened pretty often, he didn't conclude that the plan was terrible; he just recognized that the battle was.

Like every great military leader, Mao knew the difference between strategy and tactics. Strategy is the plan that takes you to your goal; tactics are what you do to carry out the strategy. Despite tactical setbacks, a great strategy often wins wars.

You can see why Kissinger admired his enemy. But Kissinger is a notoriously unsuccessful dieter. When he was secretary of state, he had three hundred suits to match his wildly fluctuating weight. Maybe Kissinger should have used Mao's wisdom at mealtime. A good strategy for weight control is to eat less junk food and to begin exercising. Some tactics would include cutting out the candy bar you have during coffee break and doing twenty sit-ups before breakfast every morning.

Three days into your weight loss plan you find yourself pumping quarters into the office candy machine. Has your diet failed? Mao wouldn't think so. He would have seen that wayward candy bar as a battlefield setback and might have recommended one of several alternatives:

✦ Eat a bit less over the next week than you initially intended.
✦ Expect to lose weight a little more slowly than you planned.
✦ Change the goal to allow a little more weight than originally planned. (Actually Mao wasn't big on changing goals, but we're no revolutionaries.)

There's only one downside to the Mao weight loss plan. The Chairman didn't see his revolution succeed until decades after he started. You may wish to see results a bit more quickly than that. Still, you get the point. The Mao technique works on anything where you need to set goals and stick to them.

Have you noticed how similar the Communist Chinese were to the early Puritans? An occasional sin or retreat doesn't prove you won't get to heaven—or to a workers' paradise. When you believe that a goal is your fate, straying becomes nothing more than a slight detour.

EXERCISE OPTIONS

I F YOU THINK YOUR BODY'S NATURAL STATE is skinnier than its current state, then the most efficient way to reform is to eat better, eat less, and combine these habits with exercise. Exercise is overrated as a sole means of losing weight. One candy bar can contain more than eight hundred calories, about two hours' worth of intense workout. It takes less time to avoid eating a candy bar than it does to work off the eight hundred calories. That's one reason why so much household exercise equipment lies around unused. People work out for a couple of weeks, get frustrated that they're not losing weight, and give up. An exercise routine can actually make you heavier; muscles are denser than fat, and the bathroom scale may not give you a cheerful report even when you're fitter.

If you're thinking about exercising more, go back to the three original body goals: health, physical abilities, and appearance. "Weighing less" is too restrictive a target. Stick to the lifetime bodily goals, use three- or six-month targets to measure progress, and you may actually hit on some exercise that doesn't feel like torture.

In Chapter 4 we talked about setting multiple targets, being happy when we met some of them, and using the information if we didn't meet any of them. Three broad categories to use for exercise targets are aerobic capacity, strength, and flexibility.

Aerobic capacity is the ability of your heart and lungs to deliver oxygen throughout your body. If you can run up several flights of stairs without getting winded, then you're in good aerobic shape. If you find yourself gasping when you walk to your car, your body isn't efficient with the oxygen you're breathing.

Strength is your muscles' ability to work the way you want them to.

As people age, they tend to lose strength faster than they lose aerobic fitness. But it takes less time to regain strength than it does to improve aerobic capacity.

Flexibility is something else you often lose with age. Can you touch the floor with both your palms while bending your knees only slightly? Then you're very flexible. Do you have trouble tying your shoes? Then you're not. Women tend to stay limber later in life than men do, but even guys can gain flexibility through regular stretching.

What does all this have to do with getting skinny? Very little, unless you combine exercise with healthful eating. By toning up various muscle groups, however, you can also make parts of your body look less flabby. You may not weigh less, but you look better.

ACCIDENTAL EXERCISE

THERE WAS A TIME when people got all the exercise they wanted, and then some, during the working day. People got paid to exercise; they walked behind plows, or carried bales of hay, or strained to pull horses out of the mud. Nowadays the couch potato is our national vegetable. Thanks to suburban developments, elevators, cars, "service" jobs, and household laborsaving devices, we don't walk, pull, or push, or lift, or climb, or even get out of chairs as much as we used to. We are an increasingly unfit nation.

Your life doesn't have to be that way. Before you sign up for another aerobics class or buy the latest-model treadmill, consider some ways you can pick up exercise here and there in your normal day:

Park far. Want to save time when you park your car at crowded places?

Uncle Tom's Aerobic Plan

HARRIET BEECHER STOWE walked twice a day for a total of five to seven miles. "If I am not feeling well, I can usually walk it off," she said. "Or, if not, I sleep it off, going to bed by eight o'clock."

Moral: Exercise and health are a better match than exercise and appearance. Mrs. Stowe is not remembered for her beauty, but she had the stamina to write some of her century's most important literature.

Don't agonize over finding a spot up close. Park a distance away and walk.

Take the stairs. Eschew the elevator whenever possible, at work, in shopping malls, at the airport, in hotels. The stairs are often faster. If the doctor says your heart is fine, begin by climbing slowly, one step at a time. After a few weeks of stair climbing, vary the routine: Take two steps occasionally, or jog some flights. Do you perspire a little? People probably won't notice. Fix yourself up in a bathroom.

Ditch the kitchen gadgets. Give away or sell electric devices. Start with the electric can opener; the manual kind is great for strengthening your grip and your wrists. Ditto for eggbeaters. Try food processing with a knife and a grater. You save money on the equipment and repairs; you save shelf space; you may even save time, since many electric kitchen tools are harder to clean than the human-powered kind; most of all, you gain upper-body strength. (A washboard instead of a washing machine would be even better, but we don't want to push things.)

Carry your own luggage. Airports are rumbling with the sound of suitcases that have casters built into them so they can be dragged like pull toys. They're clever inventions but bad exercise equipment. If you want to save your back and get fit, acquire a frameless backpack. Sporting goods stores and catalogs sell them in all sizes. Most fit in airplane overhead luggage compartments. You can carry packs hands-free, with little strain on back and shoulders. Packs don't wrinkle clothing as much as you think, and fitness research has shown that walkers get considerably more exercise with a weight on their backs.

Run your own errands. Do you have a memo for an officemate? Dash it over yourself. Instead of sending an E-mail message to someone on the next floor, pop up and talk personally. If the boss allows it, look for any excuse to get out of your chair.

Change your commute. Do you take the bus to work? Walk an extra stop or two. Do you live within several miles of your job? Try walking, running, or riding a bike. (It helps if there's a shower or at least a place to change.) If you blend exercise with commuting, you make the self-discipline part easier; it's just part of the commute.

CROSS TRAINING

SUPPOSE YOU WALKED to and from the bus stop five times a week, took the stairs instead of the elevator up three flights to your office, and went bicycling or hiking with your kids on the weekend. You would be in better shape than most Americans, fewer than half of whom get any regular exercise. You would also be practicing a technique recommended by top fitness experts, cross training. The term simply means doing more than one kind of exercise regularly. If you went jogging every weekday, your legs would probably start feeling tired by Friday. But if you swam twice a week and jogged three times a week, you'd have more energy for both. This imitates what people were bred to do naturally, a variety of things. Our Cro-

---

A Smoker Is Reborn Every Minute

⟶⟶⟶⟵⟵⟵

THE FOUNDATION OF SUCCESS IN LIFE is good health; that is the sub-
stratum of fortune; it is also the basis of happiness.
—P. T. BARNUM, who smoked ten cigars a day before he quit cold turkey

---

Magnon ancestors ran away from enemies, walked in search of food, and
carried wood. They were cross trainers.

Our hunter-gatherer ancestors practiced another form of exercise whose
benefits have only recently been discovered: long slow distance, or LSD.
Studies of middle-aged athletes show that a weekly low-key, long-lasting activity caused their weight to drop significantly. A slow jog lasting three or
four hours (they were athletes, remember) taught their bodies to convert
fat into fuel. Instead of just burning sugars, the way we usually do when
we exercise, the LSD athletes burned up fat—even during their shorter,
more intense exercises. There is every reason to believe that you can teach
your body the same trick by going on a weekly hike. A mountain a week
could provide the fat-burning lesson your body needs. If you live in flat terrain, wear a pack and try to maintain a brisk walking pace.

LSD is no substitute for other exercise. To be in your best shape, you
should do some sort of activity for twenty minutes or more, three or four
times a week. Nor is LSD alone the best way to lose weight. But the combination of good eating, a hike a week, and two or three other forms of
exercise during the workweek could take you reasonably far toward the
three goals of health, prowess, and looks.

"Reasonably?" you say. "What's so reasonable about exercising six or
seven hours a week and eating like a saint?"

Naked Ambition

JOHN QUINCY ADAMS took an occasional morning swim in the Potomac
when he was president. Once he swamped his boat and lost most of his
clothes. He walked back to the White House half naked and embarrassed.

Moral: Dignity should never get in the way of fitness. Remember Adams the
next time you feel self-conscious about exercise.

If it doesn't sound reasonable, it probably isn't for you. Not yet. The
best way to get in shape is to take your time.

PHYSICAL TARGETS

DECIDE TO GET IN SHAPE FOR THE NEXT DECADE, not the next
week. Set modest three- or six-month targets to measure your
progress. As you meet the targets, gradually up the ante.

Let's set a few sample goals and put some targets with them. In the
health category we want to stay uninjured. Our abilities goal is to get out
of bed in the morning without groaning and to be a hiker unusually late
in life. For appearance, we want to weigh about ten pounds less than we
do now and to keep that weight off forever. We also want people to think
we're ten years younger than we actually are. Or maybe twenty years
younger, by the time we're, say, ninety.

Those are the goals. Now for the targets and the training to go with
them. It's time for a table.

TARGETS

	HEALTH	ABILITIES	APPEARANCE
Three-month targets	Stay uninjured. Go three months without a cold.	Walk from bed to bathroom in the morning without staggering. Run/walk two miles. Hike four miles of an easy trail.	Lose two pounds. Fit in pants bought last year.
Six-month targets	Stay uninjured. Go six months with just one cold.	Walk easily to the bathroom in the morning. Run two miles. Hike four miles of a hilly trail.	Lose three pounds. Fit in suit bought three years ago.
One-year targets	Stay uninjured. Go one year with just two colds, no more serious illness.	Get up in the morning without feeling uncomfortably stiff. Run four miles. Hike up three-thousand-foot mountain without difficulty.	Lose five pounds. Fit in suit bought five years ago.

Setting cold prevention as a target may seem like tempting fate, but there is evidence that sustained periods of fresh air and raised body temperature really can fight colds. A strong body is less susceptible to diseases in general. At any rate, if you come down with more than two colds in a year, you can look for encouragement to other targets.

Notice that training and targets get a bit blurred in the "Abilities" column. The more exercise you get, the more you're capable of doing. This is part of the ratcheting-up phenomenon we talk about in previous chapters. A four-mile run may seem impossible at first, routine after a year or so. Let's look at a sample exercise plan, keyed to the table above. It's just a sample, mind you; a real plan should have your physician's approval and would have to be geared to your own age, abilities, goals, and schedule. Consider the table below a template for your own plan.

TRAINING

MONTHS 1–3

Aerobic Fitness	Brisk two-mile walk during lunch hour twice a week. Take stairs instead of elevator at work. Short weekend hikes with family in state park at least once a month. Two-mile walk/jog after work once a week.
Flexibility	Each Sunday morning, do stretching exercises with a videotape. Before bed every night, bend over (with knees slightly bent) and try to touch toes. Try to remember to do a bit of stretching at work.
Strength	Borrow a video from the library on calisthenics. Learn proper sit-up (or other stomach exercise) and safe push-up techniques. Install a chin-up bar in bathroom doorframe. Every night (with help of a chair if necessary), try to do one pull-up.

MONTHS 4–6

Aerobic Fitness Brisk two-mile walk during lunch hour twice a week.
Take stairs instead of elevator at work.
Weekend hikes with family in state park at least once a month.
Talk them into hillier terrain.
Two-mile jog once a week after work or on weekend.

Flexibility Do shortened version of Sunday stretching routine for ten minutes after getting out of bed every weekday morning.
Continue full stretch every Sunday.
Light stretch before bed every evening.
Try to remember to do periodic stretching at work.

Strength Every weekday morning, combine stretching with ten sit-ups or stomach crunches and ten push-ups.
Every weekday after work, do one pull-up. Try to work up to two pull-ups.

MONTHS 7–12

Aerobic Fitness Brisk two-mile walk on lunch hour twice a week.
Take stairs instead of elevator at work.
Talk family into climbing a few peaks.
Gradually increase weekly run from two to four miles.

Flexibility Get up fifteen minutes early each weekday to do stretching and strength routine.
Continue full stretch every Sunday.
Light stretch before bed every evening.
Try to remember to do periodic stretching at work.

Strength Build up to twenty sit-ups and twenty push-ups each weekday morning.
Build up to four pull-ups and three chin-ups every weekday evening.

The one-year routines above may look positively crazy, especially if you've never done regular exercise. Does it seem like a lot of time? Do the exercises seem impossible? Then don't look at the "Months 7–12" section. Look at the section for the first three months. Devote just one hour of your workweek to exercise during this period. On the weekends make sure you do something fun that lasts at least an hour—biking, hiking, skiing, swimming—anything that gets you outside and breathing. (Or inside and breathing if the weather stinks.) After a few months up the ante. You'll probably be capable of greater athletic feats. Add a short morning exercise routine. After a while this shouldn't seem the torture it looks at first. If you turn down the heat at night, a little early-morning exercise warms you up better than a shower, and it has the advantage of speeding your metabolism, allowing your body to burn more calories during the day.

By combining the right exercise and eating and by setting modest targets that gradually increase, you might surprise yourself by actually meeting some of those targets. If you meet all of them, you may have set your targets a bit low. A little failure is good for the soul.

Phil Jensen's Daily Constitutional

━➤◆◆◀━

A T SEVENTY-FOUR, Phil Jensen of Berlin, New Hampshire, climbs Mount Washington every day. He trots up the Northeast's tallest peak (6,288 feet) in ninety minutes—half the time of a normal fit person.

Moral: A high goal to one person can seem routine to another. One is resolution; the other, habit.

THE GOAL OF A NEW MACHINE

I F YOU'RE THINKING OF BUYING EXERCISE EQUIPMENT, look in your newspaper's classified listings for used stuff. Few people stick to their home equipment more than several months. To make sure you use your machinery over the long run, don't buy it until you already do at least two kinds of exercise routinely, such as running and aerobics class. Plan to use the home machine when the weather is bad or you can't get to the gym. Don't make the equipment your sole means of training; use it for cross training. The best machine employs most or all of your large-muscle groups so that you can get maximum aerobic benefit with minimal strain. A popular kind imitates cross-country skiing. It doesn't hurt your back, and it is a more rigorous workout than it feels—a high ratio of gain to pain. A rowing machine offers a similar benefit, but it can be hard on bad backs. If you travel a lot, consider packing one of the most efficient aerobic devices ever invented, a jump rope.

If your equipment doesn't come with a manual, find an explanatory book or video. Start slowly, concentrating on proper form to avoid injury. Spend ten minutes on the machine your first several times, then twenty minutes of slow movement. Increase your speed over the months until you're going as fast as you like. Then increase your time to half an hour or more.

TRAINING FOR EVENTS

S UPPOSE YOU'VE HAD a successful year of losing weight, getting stronger, and feeling younger. Your spouse looks at you with lust. Friends gossip about you. Your closet becomes a treasure chest of once-unwearable clothing. You're now ready for the big time. Like any good athlete, you can use a little competition.

You don't need other people to compete; your own targets make for good sport. All you need is an event to train for. You can make it up if necessary. "I'm in training," you can say to yourself proudly. This sounds much nobler than "I'm on a diet" or "I'm learning to jog." There is the danger that a big event can work like a diet, making you overly smug if you meet a goal. To avoid that trap, plan an event at least once a year, to give you a regular training season.

If you've never competed athletically as an adult, select an activity you'd most want to train for, such as a run, or a swim, or a mountain climb. It should seem pretty hard but doable. Get your doctor's okay first. Here are a few sample events, both organized and personal.

The two-mile Thanksgiving "turkey trot." This is a common event, often sponsored by local recreation departments or chambers of commerce. If you run four miles comfortably, this race is right for you. Establish multiple targets—for example, to complete the race in less than fifteen minutes, finish better than the bottom third of your age-group, pass at least ten people, and not feel terrible at the end. Decide to be satisfied if you meet two out of the four targets.

Begin training for the race three months ahead of time. Cut way back on alcohol. Eat like someone in training, avoiding fats and refined sugar. If you can run the racecourse, time yourself on it once in a while. Mark out a mile's road running with your car odometer. Try to set a regular pace, such as eight minutes to the mile. Increase the amount of stretching you do in the morning. Vary your workouts, running a slow and easy four miles now and then and an occasional fast two miles. One week before the race, taper your training routine, easing up on the speed and mileage so you'll be fresh on race day.

The tough mountain climb. Look in regional guidebooks for a challenging peak that you could do safely in a day. If you can comfortably climb two thousand feet in several hours, look for a hike that takes you up three thousand feet. This is not a competitive event in the sense of beating your hiking partners up the mountain; it's a more personal challenge.

Train for the event three months in advance by making sure you have properly broken-in boots or shoes with good ankle support, along with clothing that will keep you warm and dry in dramatically changing weather. Increase your aerobic exercise. Build up your legs by jogging upstairs at home or work. Establish a plan for running a certain number of flights each week. If you have the time and money, find a health club with stair-climbing machines. These impressive (and expensive) inventions let you set and measure your own pace, and they're better for the knees than regular stairs. On the weekends practice on easy mountains if you can get to them.

The big game. Is there a neighborhood basketball court where young jocks hang out? Work up to inviting yourself into a game. Or enter a health club tennis tournament or some other low-key competition in your best sport. It may not be a big deal to the people you play, but it is to you; you've trained for the competition. Practice your sport at least twice a week for three months before competing. Get into shape by setting targets for fitness, flexibility, and strength. Taper off the week before the event by easing up on the aerobics and the practice and by increasing the amount of stretching.

The family Olympics. Set aside a Saturday or Sunday three months in advance, and ask each family member to name an athletic feat. To avoid strains on family ties, establish a different feat for each member. One might attempt to do thirty push-ups, another to run two miles in fourteen minutes, still another to dance the twist through an entire Chubby Checkers recording.

Train for the event, setting interim targets. Consider posting a chart in the kitchen to show progress.

Devote part of the big day to each event, geared around each member. Reward a blue ribbon to anyone who accomplishes a stated feat. Give a red ribbon for an effort that comes within 20 percent of the goal, a yellow ribbon for a noble try. Or you could give out little gifts, such as small framed pictures (snapshots or children's drawings) of the athletes in action.

Don't feel obligated to up the athletic ante in these ways until you have already met your initial targets; a year's exercise is a good minimum. But after a while you may challenge yourself almost automatically. As you certainly know by now, we call that ratcheting up.

Low Fruit

In which the reader decides what to do and when

YOU MAY HAVE MANAGED to get through this book without having set a single goal, gained one good habit, or found a clue to your calling. Thoughts about discipline and the future can be daunting, and you may be wondering where to begin. That is what this chapter is for: to help you start simplifying.

If you were an early New Englander, you would know exactly where to begin. Your minister and your neighbors would have been helpfully informing you of your faults all your life. As for your calling, you probably inherited it, or else your father announced it when you were old enough for education or apprenticeship. Habits arose from family life and your calling. If you were literate, you might have kept a diary to assist your family and neighbors in pointing out your sins. You would have applied yourself to correcting them, decrying your worthlessness while noting with inward satisfaction that you were basically not such an evil person.

These days we don't particularly appreciate attempts to point out our faults, we might object to having our fathers announce our careers, and our habits might be in serious need of correction. So unlike a Puritan, we can't expect to launch ourselves into self-improvement programs and uncomplicate our lives right off the bat. It takes time and a couple of valuable principles, to wit:

Discover your destination; then take the easiest route. A good plan should be a relief, not a burden. In this chapter we suggest a yearlong schedule for uncovering your calling and then choosing ways to fulfill it.

Pick the low fruit first. Set out to improve what's easiest to improve. Eliminate the complications that are most happily abandoned.

A SIMPLIFYING YEAR

I F YOUR LIFE IS AN ABSOLUTE WRECK, you need something more than this book. If it is not a total mess, don't panic about improving it. Take your time. Go over the parts of the book that mean something to you. Do the exercises in Chapter 3 that interest you. Then let your thoughts percolate for at least a month. After that, set a date on your calendar for beginning your year of simplifying. Don't start during vacation; save vacation for vacation. On the other hand, your year shouldn't begin at an especially busy time. If you like to walk while you think, begin your simplifying year during the season when walking is best for you. A Saturday or Sunday makes a good starting day.

Try to mark the date on your calendar long in advance. Congratulate yourself for having accomplished a couple of simplifying tasks: reading this book and establishing a beginning simplifying date. If you have been thinking about your purpose in life and about what makes you happy, congratulate yourself again. You still have plenty of time to nail down your calling once your year begins.

Don't get nervous about that starting date. It should be the beginning not of tough times but of useful thinking. You don't have to make a big announcement about it either unless you're into announcements. Just look forward to a time when you will think about yourself.

First month: find your calling. If you haven't satisfied yourself with the exercises in Chapter 3, do them on the first weekend of your simplifying year. Think back on your childhood, and work your way up to the present. In what ways are you different from the person you consider your true self? How much trouble would it take to eliminate the obstacles in the way of that "fate"?

You can do an additional exercise that New Englanders of the nineteenth century adored: Write your own obituary. How would you want your life summed up? "Movie Buff Suffers Fatal Stroke in Mansion Built by Successful, Adoring Children"? "Nonagenarian a Casualty of Bungee Accident"? Well, let's be serious about this. What can you realistically hope for in a summation? What accomplishments, private and public, would you most want listed? What lasting effect, however small, would you want to have on the world? Your obituary can't say everything about you, but if you write it yourself, it can help describe what your life means to you.

In a similar exercise, try describing your ideal death scene. Victorian New Englanders went nuts over such morbid stuff. Do you picture your death as heroic, as a quiet summation, as a family event? Imagine the circumstances beyond the scene itself. Are you leaving a good estate to loved ones, a life with few regrets? How can you arrange for the estate? What regrets need avoiding?

If only you really could read the ending, like flipping through to the last

The Paperback Rights
Would Be Disputed, Though

⇒●⇐

B ENJAMIN FRANKLIN was only twenty-two when he wrote his famous
epitaph, which never actually found its way onto his tombstone:

The Body of
B Franklin Printer,
(Like the Cover of an old Book
Its Contents torn out
And stript of its Lettering & Gilding)
Lies here, Food for Worms,
But the Work shall not be lost;
For it will, (as he believ'd) appear once more,
In a new and more elegant Edition
Revised and corrected,
By the Author.

Moral: Some people believe in self-improvement even after death.

page of a mystery novel. But you don't really want to do that anyway, do
you? Besides, you're helping to write the book. Naturally you will want to
imagine the happiest possible ending. How would you sum up a simple,
happy life? Employ the first six chapters in this book. What burdens of
fashion or unnecessary duty can you jettison to lighten your life? What
obstacles to your fate can you most easily eliminate? What new habits do
you need?

Nice Endings

Clara Barton's last words: "Let me go! Let me go!"

Daniel Webster's last words: "I still live." (It was engraved on popular Sheffield razors.)

John Adams's last words: "Thomas Jefferson survives."

Harriet Beecher Stowe's last words: "I love you."

The last words of William Brattle, Loyalist general during the Revolution and famous epicure: "Set the plate by for dinner."

P. T. Barnum didn't need last words. When he took to his deathbed in 1891, the New York *Evening Sun* ran his obituary early so he could read it before he died.

Moral: The end of a well-founded calling can be immortality.

The exercises should offer faint hints that get stronger as you go, until you can clearly hear what you have set out to hear, which is your calling.

Second month: goal setting. Your goals should arise directly from your ideal fate. If only one goal compels you, fine. If you come up with several, so much the better. You do not want to complicate your life with an excess of goals, but if you set three, or four at the most, they can complement each other. Pride in one accomplishment prepares you for another. Any goal that gains you time, energy, or home comfort can make other goals seem doable. Talk to your family about how your aspirations might affect them. Set goals for yourself, not for others. Few people are less bearable than those with exciting plans for improving their friends and loved ones. That is one Puritan trait you may not want to emulate.

In considering goals for yourself, review Chapters 8 through 13, and establish some broad categories. Here are some samples :

Simplify relations with my partner.
Simplify relations with my community and friends.
Simplify relations with my kids.
Become happy with what I own.
Become happy with my work.
Enjoy my free time more.
Become happy with my body.

Which is most important to you? Which is most out of sync with your calling? Now get more specific: What in these categories most needs fixing? With your partner, your goal might be to spend more quiet time; with your friends, social time; with your kids, quantity time. To become happy with what you own, you might consider two or three goals: shedding some possessions, finding the means to acquire others. In the free time category, you might be saying to yourself, "What free time?" In that case the goal could be to acquire some. For the body category, you can decide what is your real, fated physique and set goals that prove it. They might include losing weight, becoming a good walker, feeling less stiff in the morning, or attaining serious athletic prowess. Don't attach specific numbers to any of your goals. That's what targets are for, as we described them in Chapter 4.

The next step is to set your satisfaction levels. How little of your goal can you meet and still feel happy about it? How much effort would it realistically take to reach that state? Is the effort worth it? In other words, is your life simpler if you work toward your goal or if you skip the whole thing? If you wish you were skinnier, for example, the question is whether your plumpness is messing up your life enough to make it worth your while to change your eating habits and start some serious exercise. If you're considering a goal to change jobs, would the hunt disrupt your family life? Or would it be simpler to stay where you are and declare yourself satisfied?

Third through sixth month: experimenting. Once your goals are set, you will want to establish targets to measure success. But first

Persistence Equals IQ

⇥

"**G**ENIUS IS INFINITE patience," said Michelangelo. This was one of Louisa May Alcott's favorite quotations.

you must establish a baseline of measurement. Spend several months doing research on your goal: what you think it will take to achieve it; the size and scope of the obstacles in your way; the habits and skills you need. On some goals, plot samples come in handy. Here are various ways you can measure yourself, culled from the other chapters in this book and matched with goal categories:

GOAL CATEGORY	MEASUREMENTS
Possessions (Chapter 10)	Moot move
	Household plot sample
Work (Chapter 11)	Research education needed for a job
	Background research on employers
Rest (Chapter 12)	Counting seconds with and without watch
	Analyzing vacations you've taken
Body (Chapter 13)	Consulting a doctor about fitness routines
	Week's diet plot sample

You can "measure" where you stand with spouse and children as well. Examine the times you or your kids have become angry. Think of how you handled an argument with your partner. How could you have done better? Your behavior is your baseline. How you wish you behaved can be a target.

This period can also give you a chance to scope out potential mentors, as we discussed in Chapter 8. Is there someone who seems especially accomplished in a category you want to improve? Talk to the person. Ask for advice. Get her to share the ways she screwed up as well as her successes. Besides being educational, the failure of a superior is reassuring to the rest of us. If you don't feel comfortable talking to your chosen mentor, watch him or her from afar.

Seventh through ninth month: habituating and sloughing. This is the crucial simplifying period, when you begin to get rid of complications and obstacles. During these three months you work on time and habits.

+ Look at Chapter 6 for ways to find pockets of time. You can free up hours for your goals or see the extra time as a goal in itself.
+ Get rid of social obligations that don't satisfy you and have little to do with your calling. See our advice on learning to say no.
+ Decide how much time you want to carve from your television habits.
+ If you can get yourself up at five every morning, you have something in common with history's most admirable New Englanders. Consider following our plan for changing your wake-up time in the fall.
+ Examine your commuting time, and see if some of it can't be spent on your goals.

Next, set habits specific to the individual goals. Begin sloughing off the ones you don't want, and acquire those most useful for meeting your targets. Remember, start with what's easiest, do what most readily becomes automatic. See the individual chapters for suggested habits.

One obstacle to toss aside is unrealistic expectations. Ditch the hopes of becoming a millionaire; establish habits that let you live like one. Forget looking like a bodybuilder (unless that's a specific, realistic goal you have set). Instead, set habits of mind and body that allow you to be satisfied with your truest physique.

Tenth through twelfth month: measuring and ratcheting. This is the time to repeat the measurements you made before you established

---

Henry Adams Knew
When to Hold 'Em

HENRY ADAMS GAVE SOME INGENIOUS ADVICE on fate in his autobiography, *The Education of Henry Adams*. "Whether life was an honest game of chance, or whether the cards were marked and forced," he wrote about himself, "he could not refuse to play his excellent hand. He could never make the usual plea of irresponsibility. He accepted the situation as though he had been a party to it, and under the same circumstances would do it again, the more readily for knowing the exact values. To his life as a whole he was a consenting, contracting party and partner from the moment he was born to the moment he died."

Moral: In joining your fate, you are a consenting adult. This may not be completely true, but it is a good attitude.

A Sample Year of Simplifying

H ERE IS WHAT A PLAN for a year of simplifying might look like for a woman with husband, career, and children:

May. Simplifying year begins. I reread the first several chapters of this book. I write my obituary and a description of my much-mourned death. I describe my calling: to be an accomplished outdoorswoman, a skilled professional, and a good wife and mother. I spend the month testing it. Is this really my destiny?

June. I set goals: to keep up with my husband in hiking the Presidential Range in New Hampshire; to learn to paddle a canoe in mild whitewater; to improve the time we spend together as a family; to quit my job and become an independent consultant working out of my home.

July–September. I hike two small peaks with a backpack, timing myself by the mile to establish a baseline for progress. I call my friend, an experienced outdoorswoman, for advice on gear. I research canoeing clinics. I discuss with family how many times a week we could realistically have dinner together. I do a plot sample of household income and expenses. I say yes to helping with Green-Up Day, no to a second term as a library trustee.

October–December. I begin getting up at 5:00 A.M. I do a morning exercise routine. I make preparations for dinner. I spend an hour each morning working on consulting assignments. I limit television to an hour each evening.

January. I go on a New Year's walk with husband. I rethink goals. I do another household plot sample. I use the neighborhood health club's annual open house to test my fitness on a stair-climbing machine. I reset new targets for March. I plan year's vacations, goals for family play time.

February. I keep it up!

March. I do the first mountain climb of the season. I attend a weekend canoe clinic in an indoor pool. As part of spring cleaning, I do a moot move. I plan a financial retreat with husband. Main topic: Can we shift some of children's college savings into expenses so I can quit my job?

April. I do an easy whitewater paddle with husband.

May. I celebrate successes. I plan moments of excess. I set higher targets. I rethink goals.

your first targets. Account for what worked and what didn't. Where you have succeeded, ratchet up by setting new targets. Where you have failed, lower your expectations.

At the end of the year congratulate yourself on the ways you have simplified your life. You should have a sense of control you never had before. You are pursuing your calling.

We hear much talk about "self-esteem," a term that would have made our predecessors in New England nervous. To esteem yourself smacks of pride, one of the worst of sins. To think too much of yourself could be proof that you aren't one of the elect after all and so have no reason for self-esteem in the first place.

And yet (with the Puritans there always was an "and yet"), as unworthy as the early believers seemed in the eyes of their God, they appeared just a bit more worthy than all the other sinners. Underneath the vaunted humility of the Puritan saints was the conviction that they were among God's chosen people. Over the generations this attitude sometimes lapsed into smugness and real snobbery. But there is a lesson for all of us in the Puritans' inner sense of worth: We can quietly hold the feeling that we are capable of setting somewhat higher standards for ourselves than may be expected of us. If you actually believe in improving yourself, in making decisions that simplify your life, you already stand apart from most people. If you act on those decisions and set goals and accompanying habits, you probably can expect to improve. The more you improve, the more you will discover the faults and complications that need fixing. But you might also begin to see yourself as chosen for a noble calling, which is your life.

You may never have lived in New England, but if you have found your calling, you have found simplicity. You are now the Yankee-est of Yankees.

Index